SUPER EASY SONGBOOK

PEACEFUL MELODIES

ISBN 978-1-70514-034-5

Visit Hal Leonard Online at
www.halleonard.com

Contact us:
Hal Leonard
7777 West Bluemound Road
Milwaukee, WI 53213
Email: info@halleonard.com

In Europe, contact:
Hal Leonard Europe Limited
42 Wigmore Street
Marylebone, London, W1U 2RN
Email: info@halleonardeurope.com

In Australia, contact:
Hal Leonard Australia Pty. Ltd.
4 Lentara Court
Cheltenham, Victoria, 3192 Australia
Email: info@halleonard.com.au

Welcome to the *Super Easy Songbook* series!

This unique collection will help you play your favorite songs quickly and easily. Here's how it works:

- Play the simplified melody with your right hand. Letter names appear inside each note to assist you.

- There are no key signatures to worry about! If a sharp ♯ or flat ♭ is needed, it is shown beside the note each time.

- There are no page turns, so your hands never have to leave the keyboard.

- If two notes are connected by a tie ⌣, hold the first note for the combined number of beats. (The second note does not show a letter name since it is not re-struck.)

- Add basic chords with your left hand using the provided keyboard diagrams. Chord voicings have been carefully chosen to minimize hand movement.

- The left-hand rhythm is up to you, and chord notes can be played together or separately. Be creative!

- If the chords sound muddy, move your left hand an octave* higher. If this gets in the way of playing the melody, move your right hand an octave higher as well.

  * *An octave spans eight notes. If your starting note is C, the next C to the right is an octave higher.*

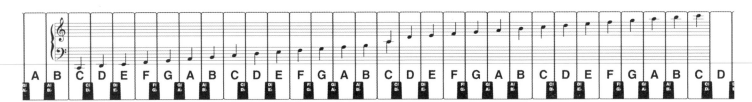
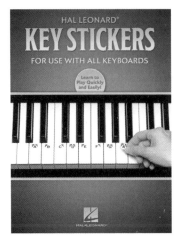

Abide with Me

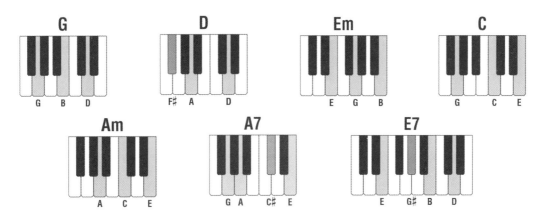

Words by Henry F. Lyte
Music by William H. Monk

Prayerfully

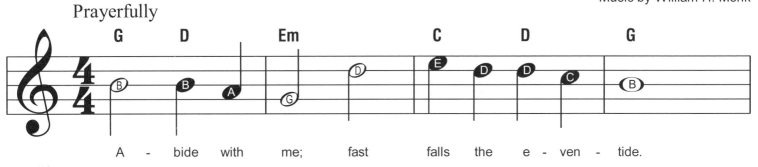

A - bide with me; fast falls the e - ven - tide.

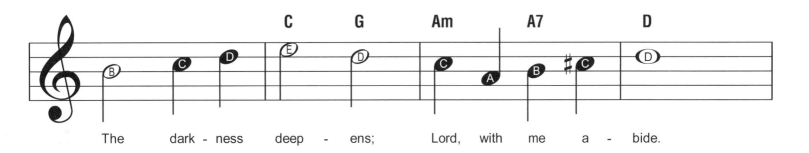

The dark - ness deep - ens; Lord, with me a - bide.

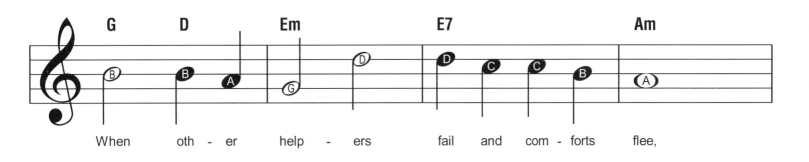

When oth - er help - ers fail and com - forts flee,

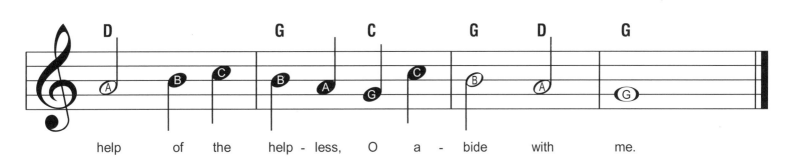

help of the help - less, O a - bide with me.

Beautiful Dreamer

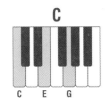
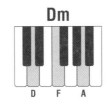
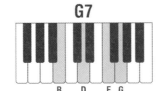
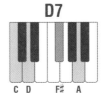
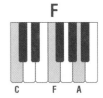

Words and Music by
Stephen C. Foster

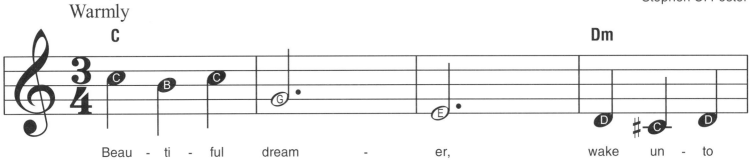

Beau - ti - ful dream - er,   wake un - to

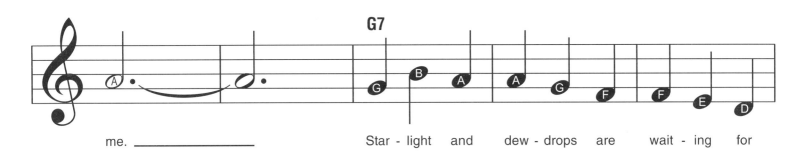

me. _____   Star - light and dew - drops are wait - ing for

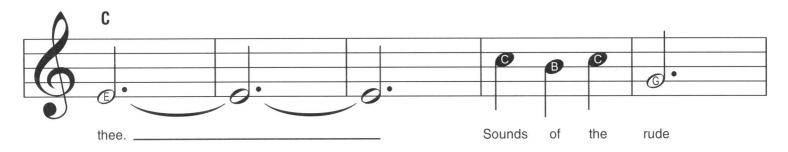

thee. _____   Sounds of the rude

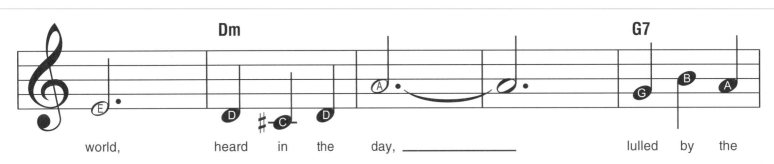

world,   heard in the day, _____   lulled by the

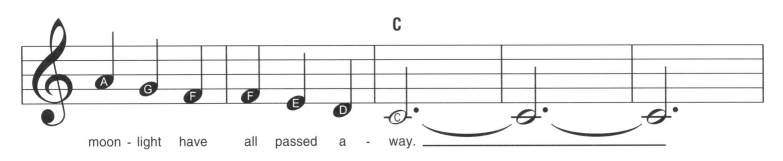

moon - light have all passed a - way. _____

Beauty and the Beast

from BEAUTY AND THE BEAST

Music by Alan Menken
Lyrics by Howard Ashman

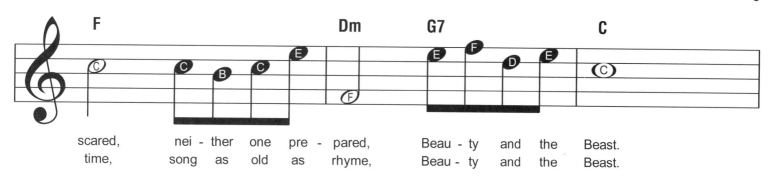

scared, nei - ther one pre - pared, Beau - ty and the Beast.
time, song as old as rhyme, Beau - ty and the Beast.

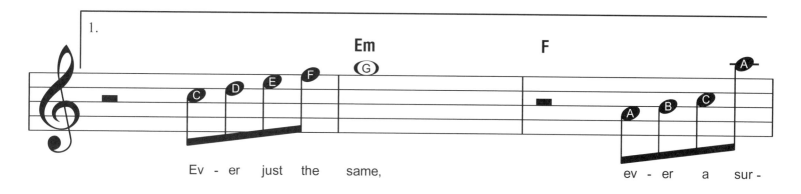

1.

Ev - er just the same, ever a sur -

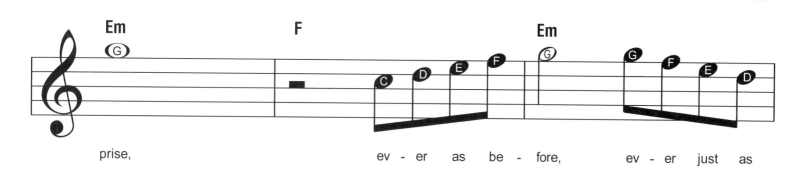

prise, ev - er as be - fore, ev - er just as

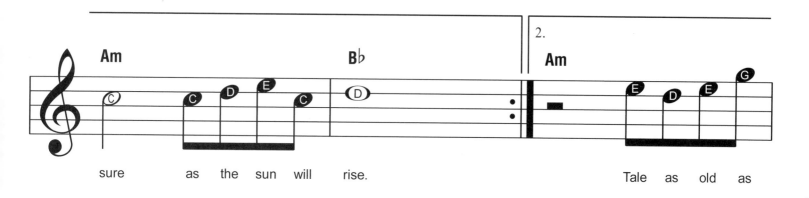

2.

sure as the sun will rise. Tale as old as

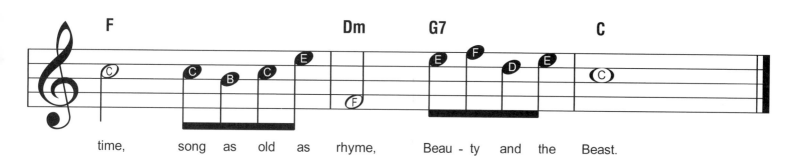

time, song as old as rhyme, Beau - ty and the Beast.

Blowin' in the Wind

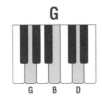
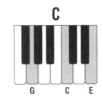
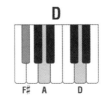
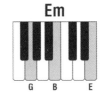

Words and Music by
Bob Dylan

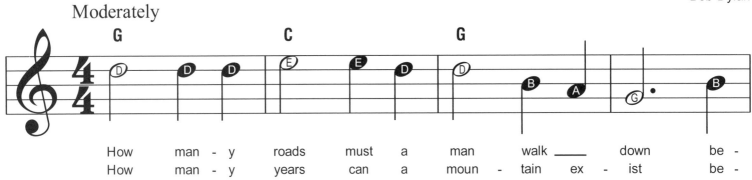

How man-y roads must a man walk ___ down be-
How man-y years can a moun-tain ex-ist be-

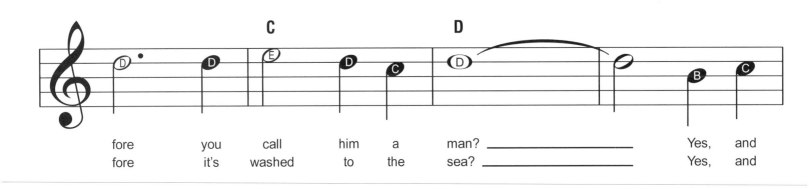

fore you call him a man? ___ Yes, and
fore it's washed to the sea? ___ Yes, and

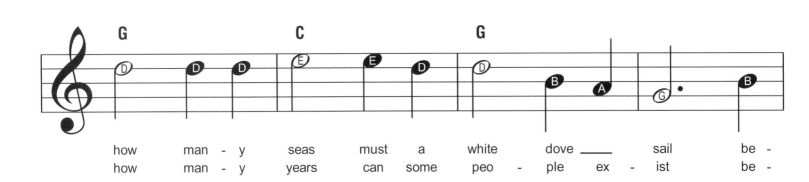

how man-y seas must a white dove ___ sail be-
how man-y years can some peo-ple ex-ist be-

11

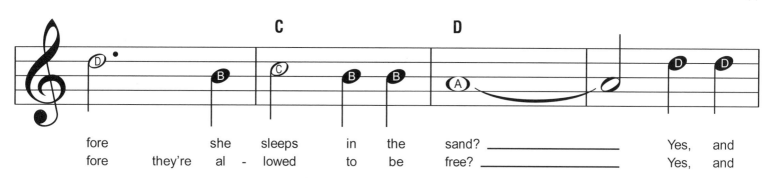

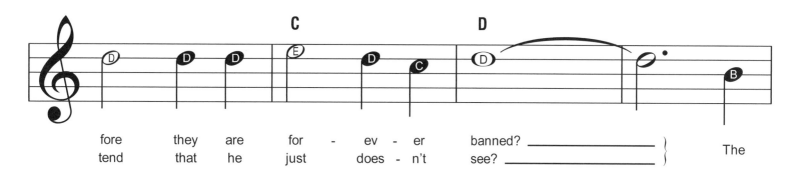

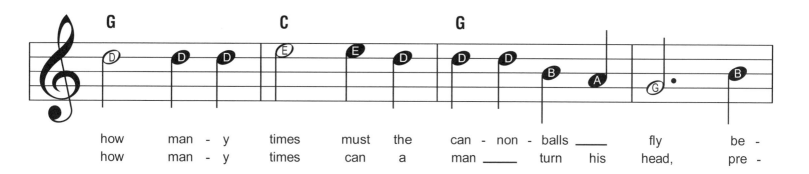

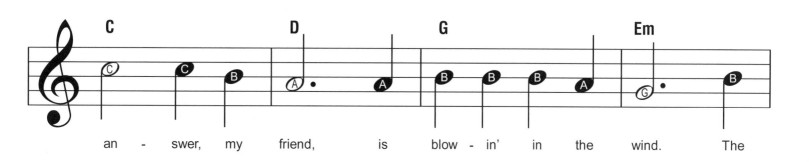

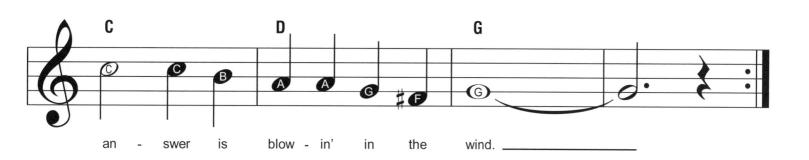

Bring Him Home

from LES MISÉRABLES

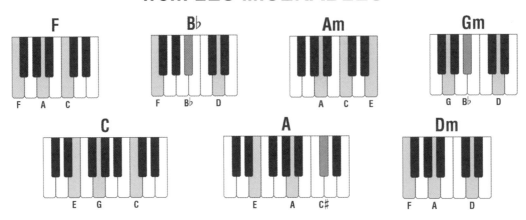

Music by Claude-Michel Schönberg
Lyrics by Herbert Kretzmer and Alain Boublil

With much expression

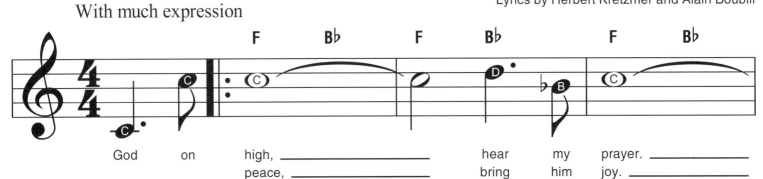

God on high, _____ hear my prayer. _____
peace, _____ bring him joy. _____

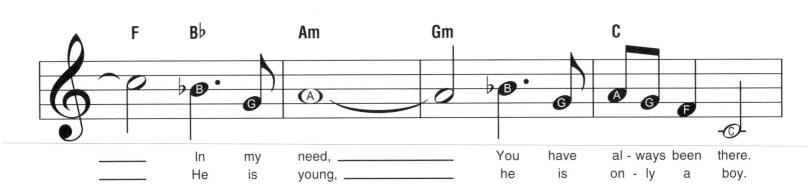

_____ In my need, _____ You have al - ways been there.
He is young, _____ he is on - ly a boy.

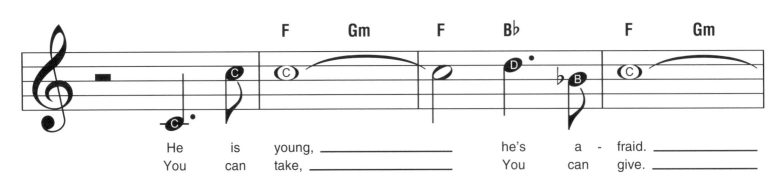

He is young, _____ he's a - fraid. _____
You can take, _____ You can give. _____

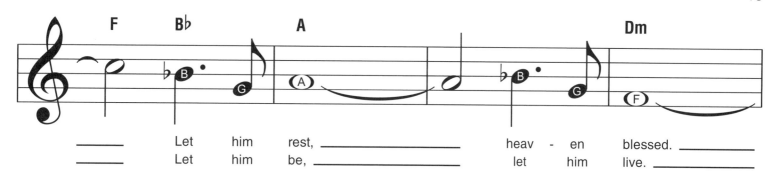

Let him rest, _____ heav - en blessed. _____
Let him be, _____ let him live. _____

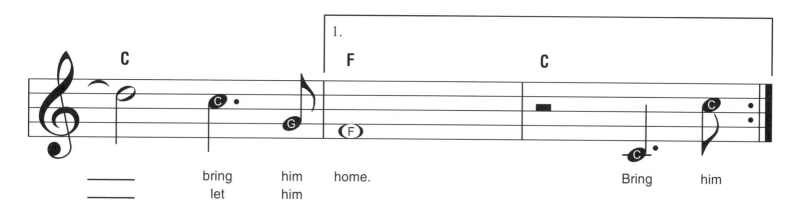

Bring him home, _____ bring him home, _____
If I die, _____ let me die, _____

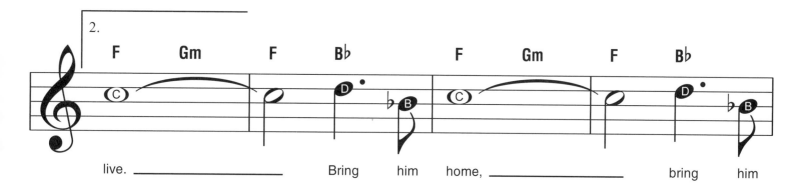

1.
_____ bring him home.
let him

Bring him

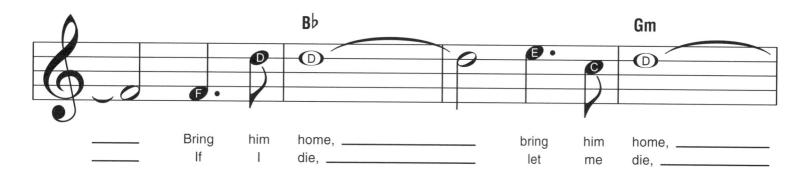

2.
live. _____ Bring him home, _____ bring him

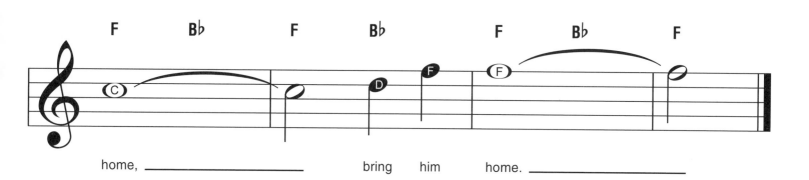

home, _____ bring him home. _____

Candle on the Water
from PETE'S DRAGON

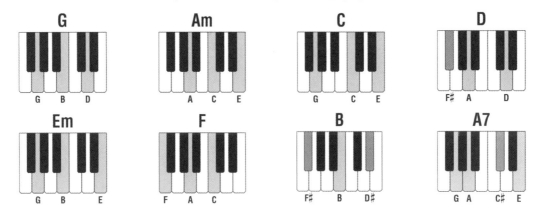

Words and Music by Al Kasha
and Joel Hirschhorn

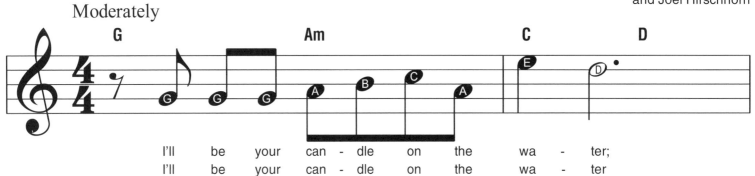

Moderately

I'll be your can - dle on the wa - ter;
I'll be your can - dle on the wa - ter

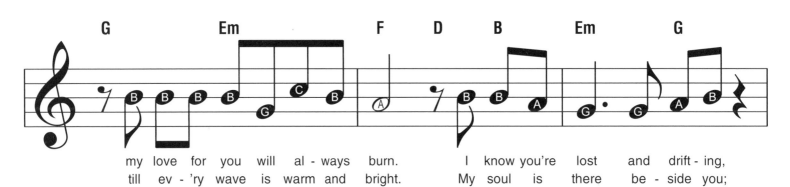

my love for you will al - ways burn. I know you're lost and drift - ing,
till ev - 'ry wave is warm and bright. My soul is there be - side you;

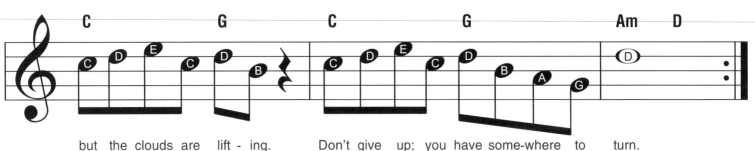

but the clouds are lift - ing. Don't give up; you have some-where to turn.
let this can - dle guide you. Soon you'll see a gold - en stream of light.

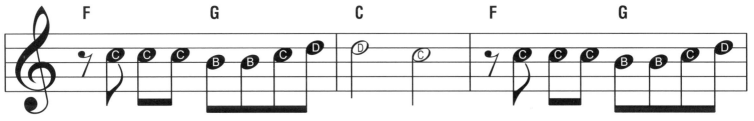

A cold and friend-less tide has found you. Don't let the storm - y dark-ness

15

Castle on a Cloud
from LES MISÉRABLES

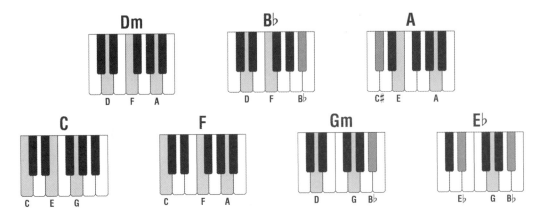

Music by Claude-Michel Schönberg
Lyrics by Alain Boublil,
Jean-Marc Natel and Herbert Kretzmer

Gently

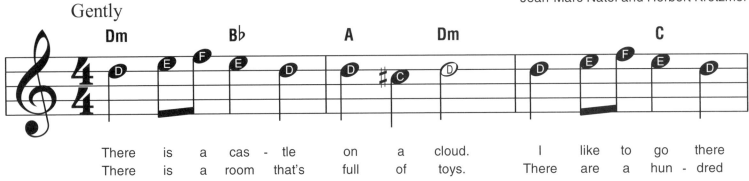

There is a cas - tle on a cloud. I like to go there
There is a room that's full of toys. There are a hun - dred

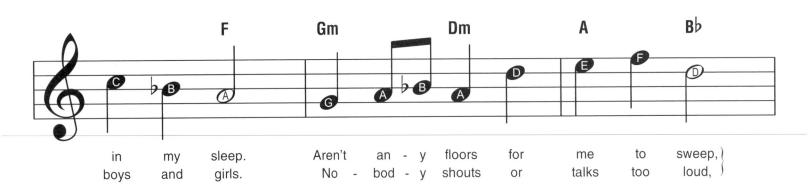

in my sleep. Aren't an - y floors for me to sweep,
boys and girls. No - bod - y shouts or talks too loud,

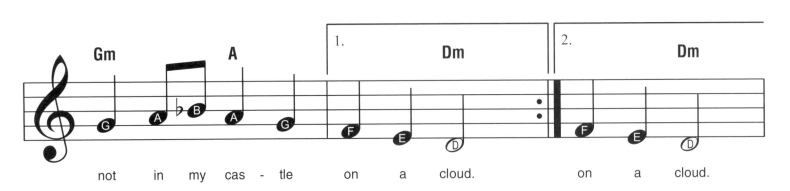

not in my cas - tle on a cloud. on a cloud.

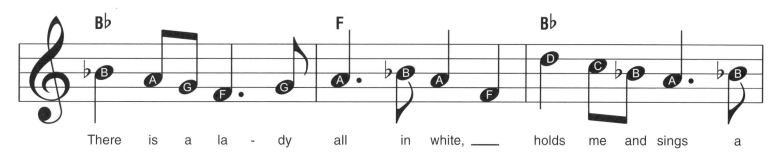

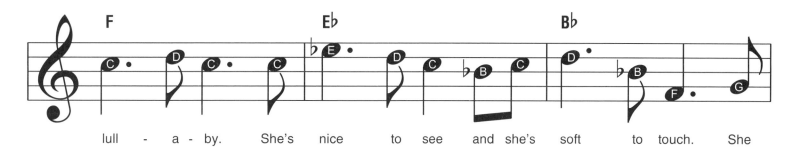

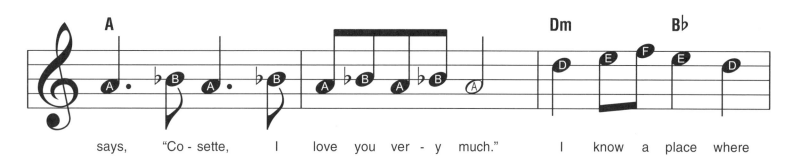

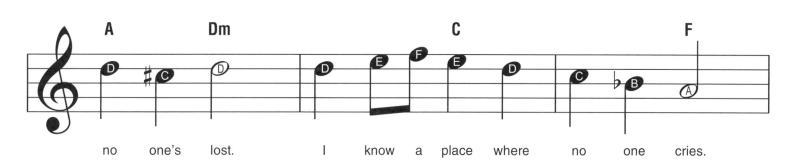

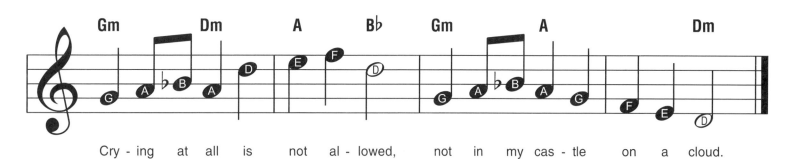

Danny Boy

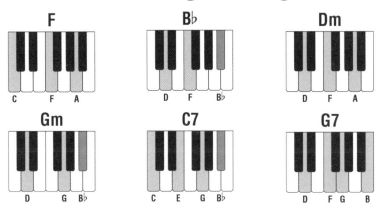

Words by Frederick Edward Weatherly
Traditional Irish Folk Melody

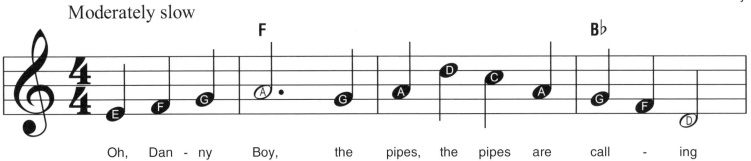

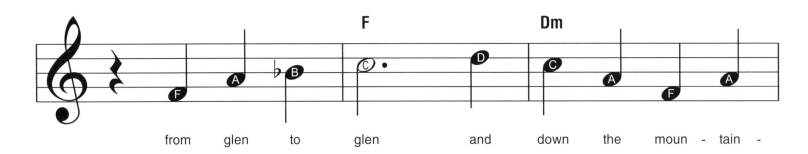

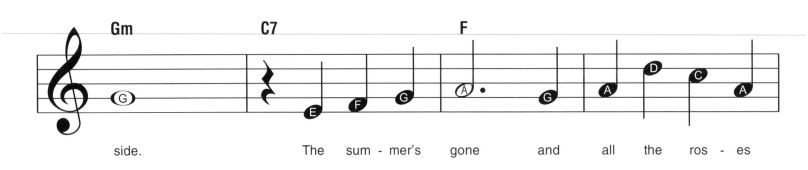

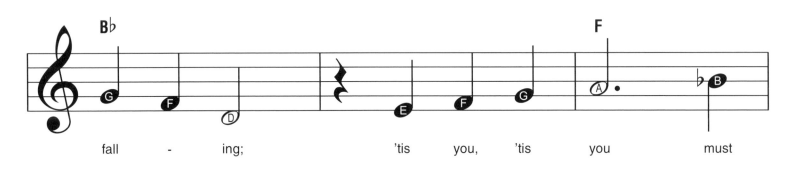

Desperado

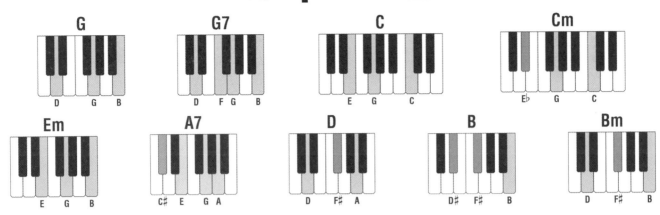

Words and Music by Don Henley
and Glenn Frey

Slow half-time feel

Des - per - a - do,　　why don't ___ you　come　to　your　sens -
　　　　　　a - do,　　oh, you ___ ain't　get - tin'　no　young -

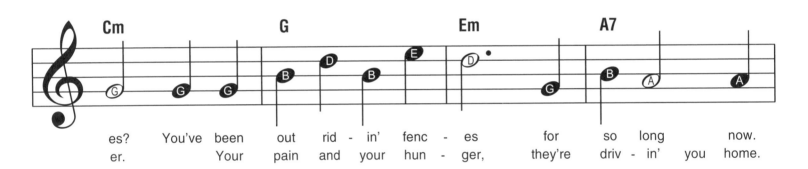

es?　You've been　out　rid - in'　fenc - es　for　so　long　now.
er.　Your　pain　and　your　hun - ger,　they're　driv - in'　you　home.

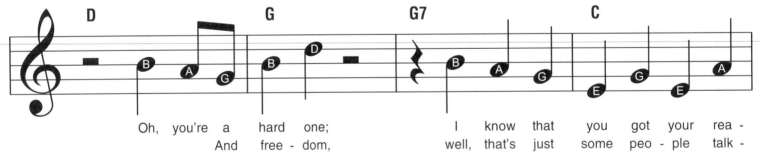

To Coda ⊕

Oh, you're a　hard　one;　I　know　that　you　got　your　rea -
And　free - dom,　well, that's　just　some　peo - ple　talk -

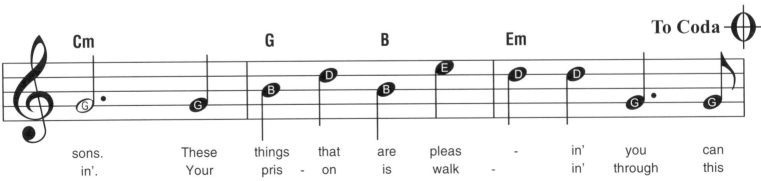

sons.　These　things　that　are　pleas - in'　you　can
in'.　Your　pris - on　is　walk - in'　through　this

Don't Know Why

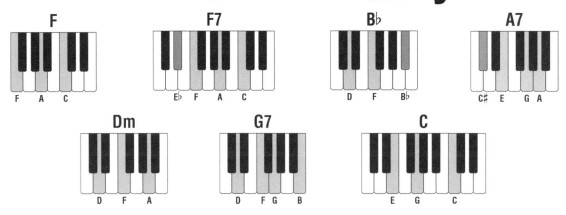

Words and Music by
Jesse Harris

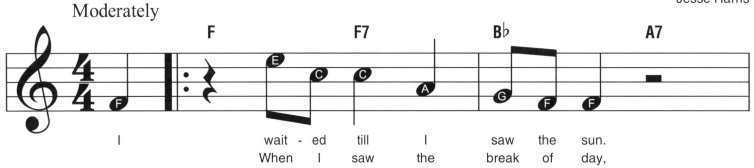

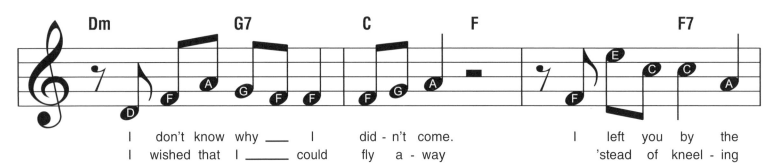

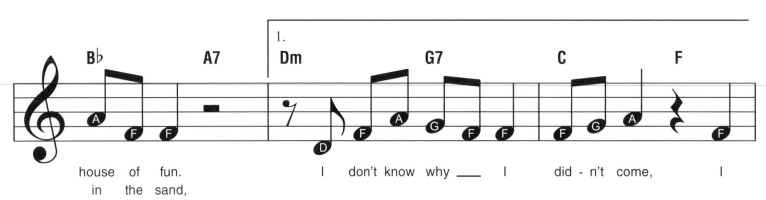

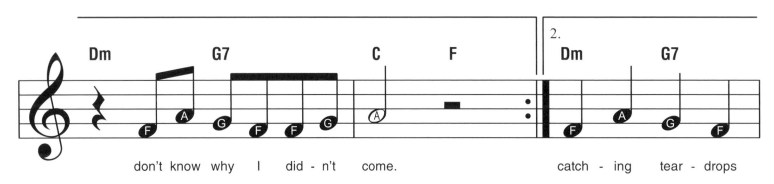

23

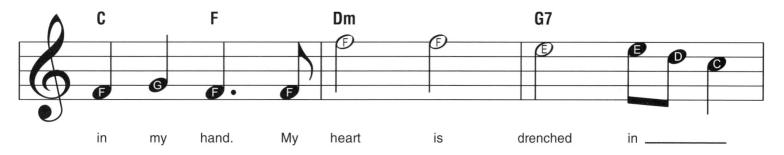

in my hand. My heart is drenched in _____

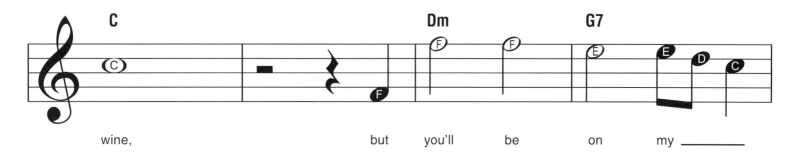

wine, but you'll be on my _____

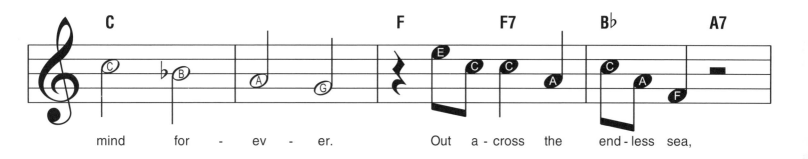

mind for - ev - er. Out a - cross the end - less sea,

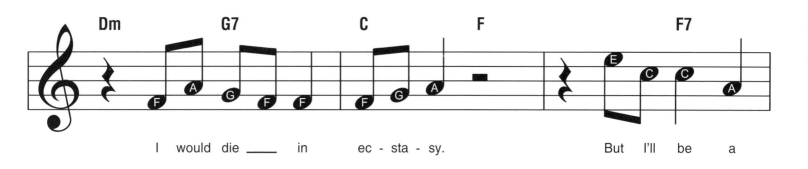

I would die ___ in ec - sta - sy. But I'll be a

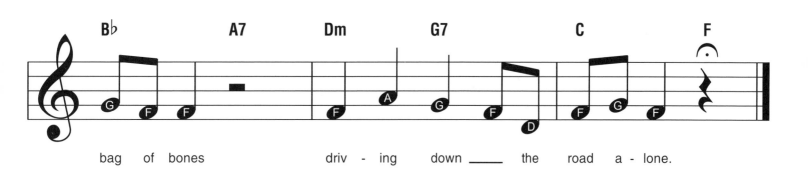

bag of bones driv - ing down ___ the road a - lone.

Edelweiss
from THE SOUND OF MUSIC

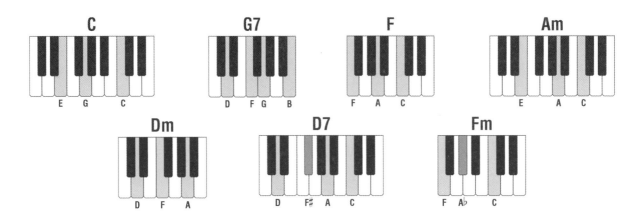

Lyrics by Oscar Hammerstein II
Music by Richard Rodgers

Simple Waltz

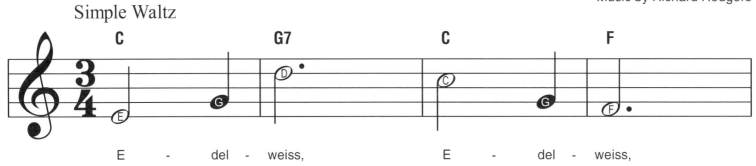

E - del - weiss,   E - del - weiss,

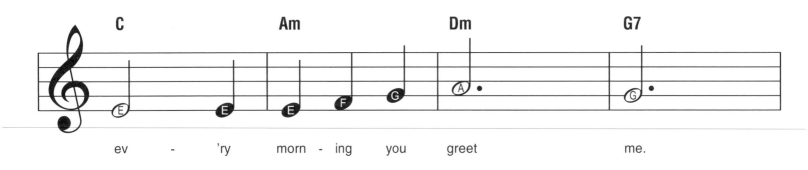

ev - 'ry   morn - ing   you   greet   me.

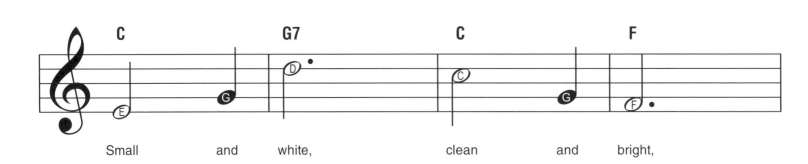

Small   and   white,   clean   and   bright,

25

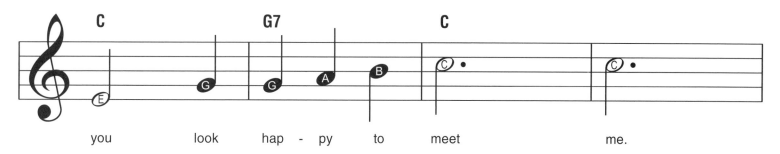

you   look   hap - py   to   meet   me.

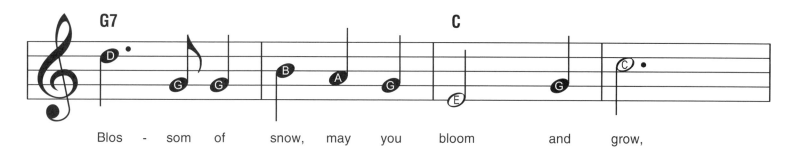

Blos - som of   snow, may you bloom   and   grow,

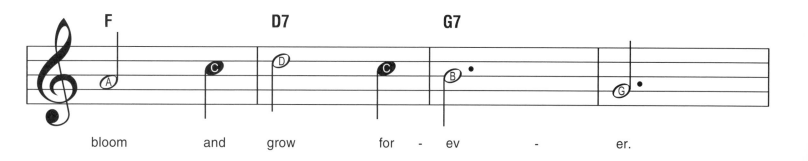

bloom   and   grow   for - ev -   er.

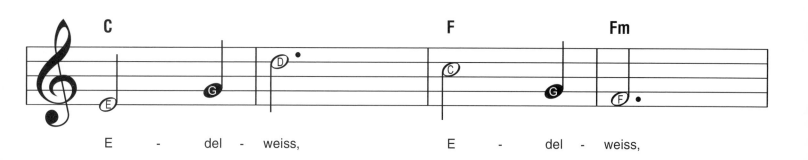

E - del - weiss,   E - del - weiss,

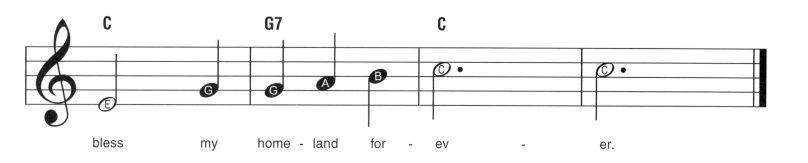

bless   my   home - land for - ev -   er.

Fix You

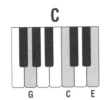
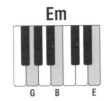

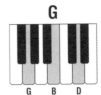

Words and Music by Guy Berryman,
Jon Buckland, Will Champion
and Chris Martin

Moderately slow

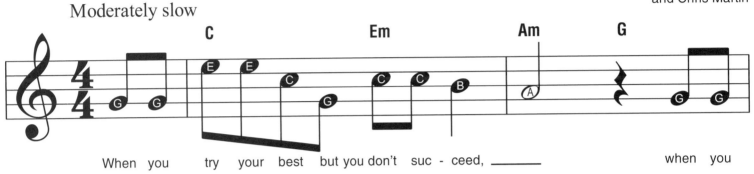

When you try your best but you don't suc - ceed, _____ when you

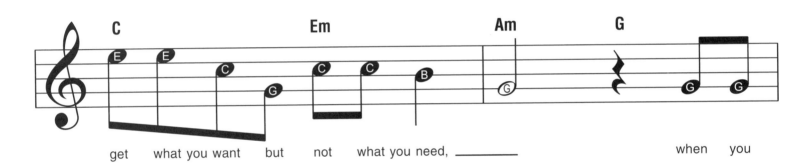

get what you want but not what you need, _____ when you

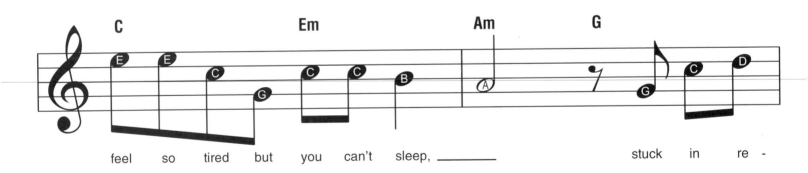

feel so tired but you can't sleep, _____ stuck in re -

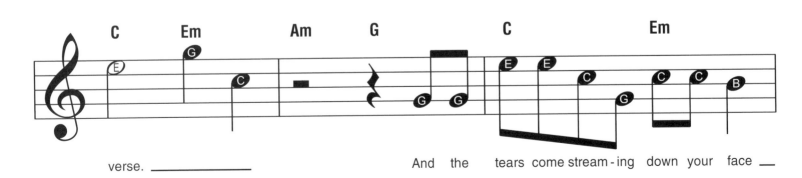

verse. _____ And the tears come stream-ing down your face _____

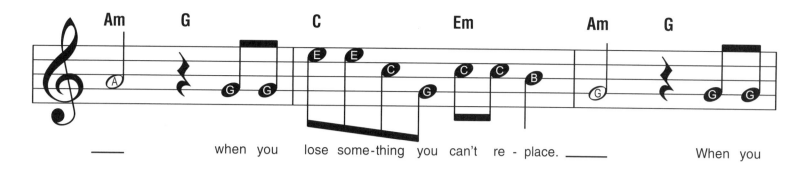

_____ when you lose some-thing you can't re - place. _____ When you

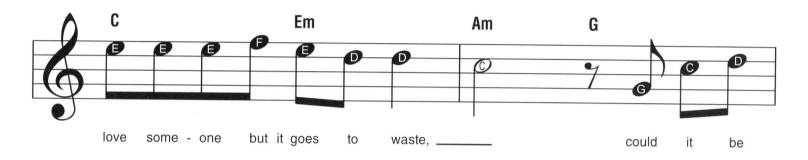

love some - one but it goes to waste, _____ could it be

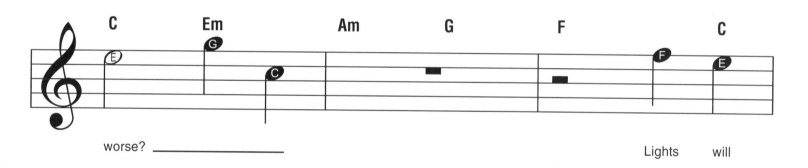

worse? _____ Lights will

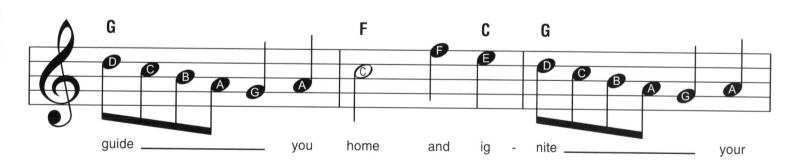

guide _____ you home and ig - nite _____ your

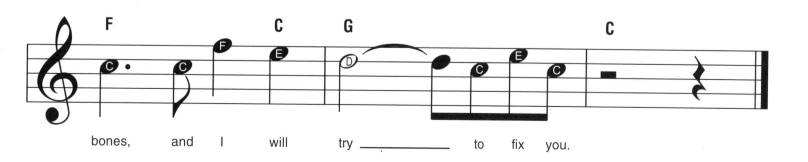

bones, and I will try _____ to fix you.

From a Distance

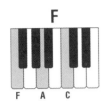 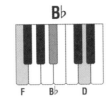 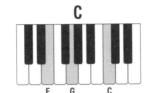 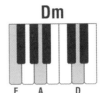 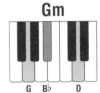

Words and Music by
Julie Gold

Moderately slow

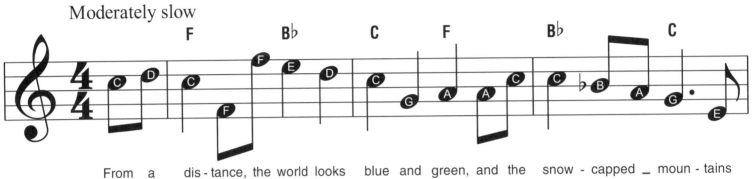

From a dis - tance, the world looks blue and green, and the snow - capped _ moun - tains

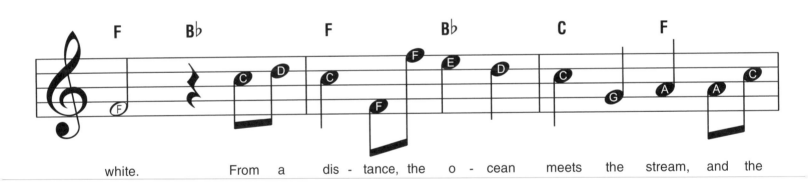

white. From a dis - tance, the o - cean meets the stream, and the

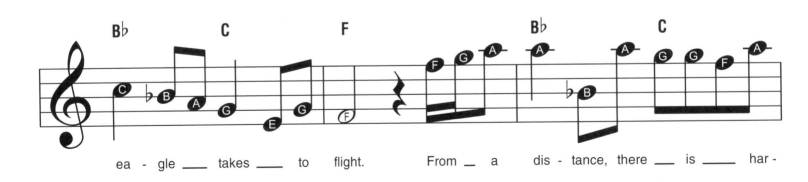

ea - gle _ takes _ to flight. From _ a dis - tance, there _ is _ har -

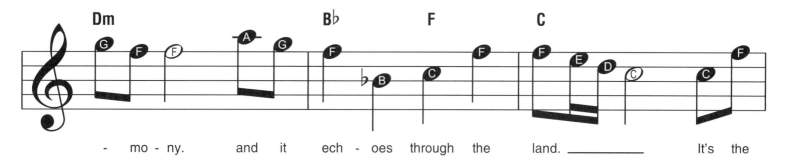

- mo - ny.   and it ech - oes through the   land. _____   It's the

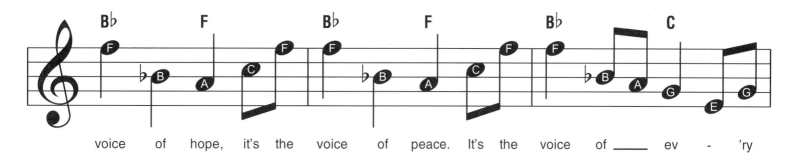

voice of hope,   it's the   voice of   peace.   It's the   voice of ____ ev - 'ry

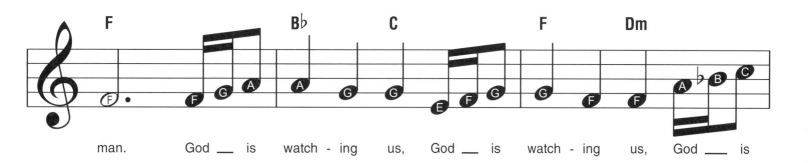

man.   God __ is watch - ing us,   God __ is watch - ing us,   God __ is

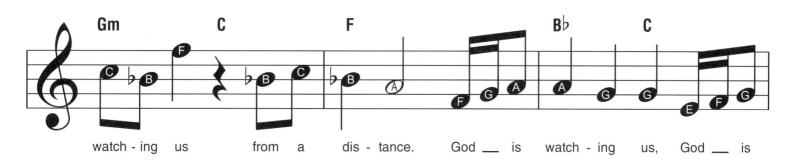

watch - ing us   from a dis - tance.   God __ is watch - ing us,   God __ is

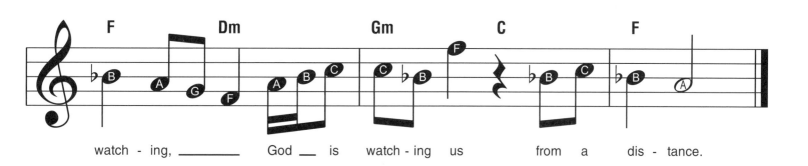

watch - ing, _____   God __ is watch - ing us   from a dis - tance.

Goodnight, My Someone

from Meredith Willson's THE MUSIC MAN

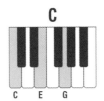
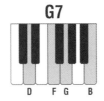
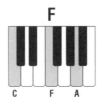
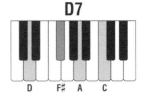

By Meredith Willson

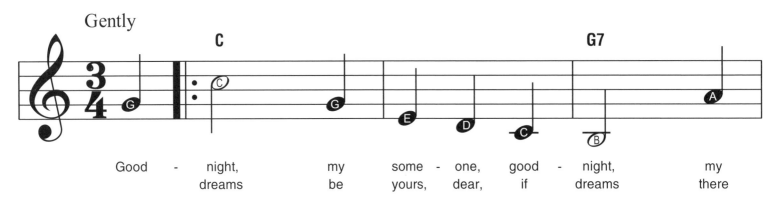

Good - night, my some - one, good - night, my
dreams be yours, dear, if dreams my there

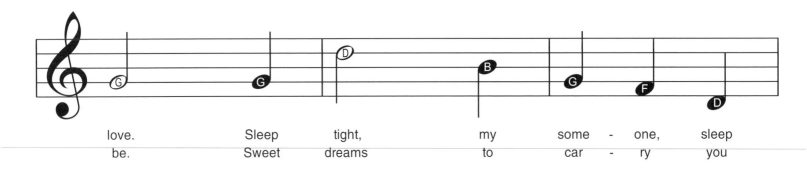

love. Sleep tight, my some - one, sleep
be. Sweet dreams to car - ry you

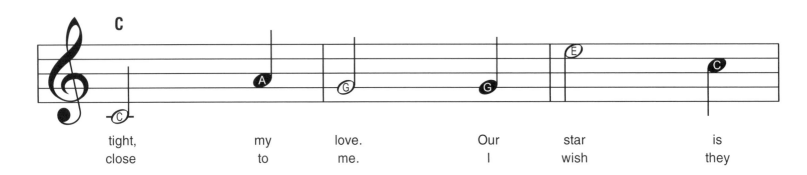

tight, my love. Our star is
close to me. I wish they

shin - ing   its   bright - est   light   for   good -
may   and   I   wish   they   might.   Now,   good -

night,   my   love,   for   good - night. _____
night,   my

1.

2.

_____   Sweet   some - one,   good - night.

Good - night,   good -

night,   good - night. _____

How Does a Moment Last Forever

from BEAUTY AND THE BEAST (2017)

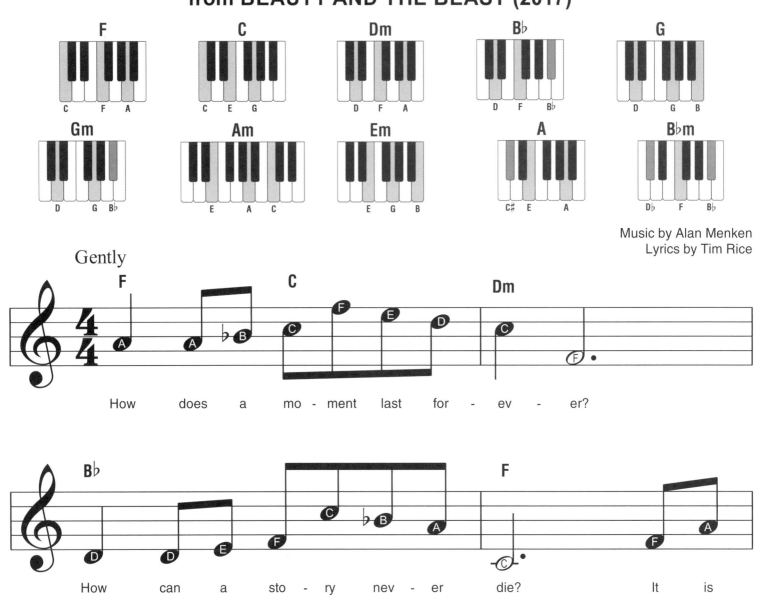

Music by Alan Menken
Lyrics by Tim Rice

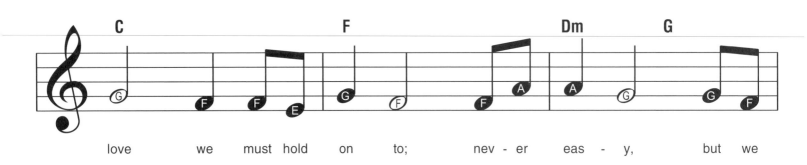

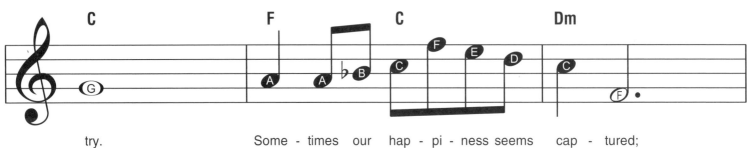

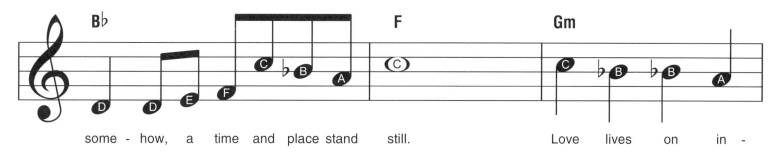

some - how, a time and place stand still. Love lives on in -

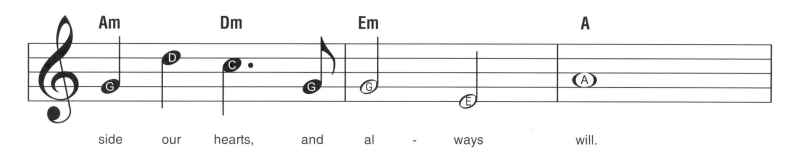

side our hearts, and al - ways will.

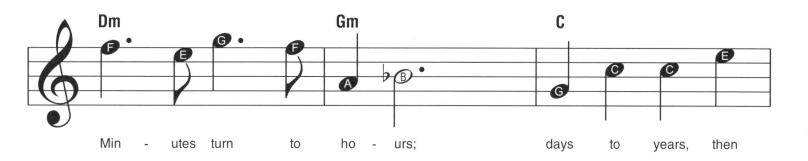

Min - utes turn to ho - urs; days to years, then

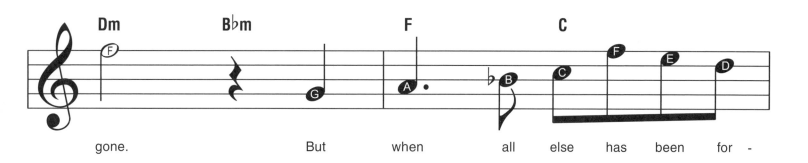

gone. But when all else has been for -

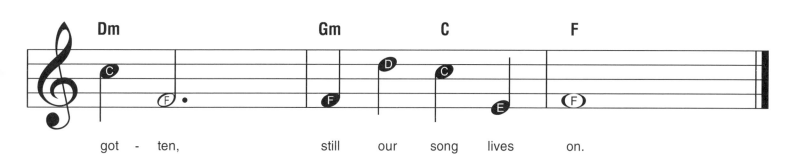

got - ten, still our song lives on.

I Dreamed a Dream
from LES MISÉRABLES

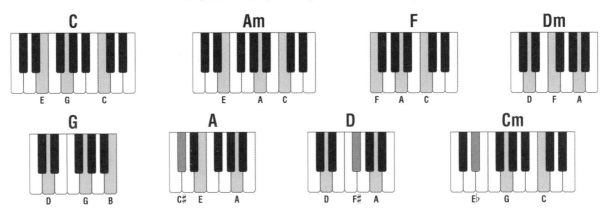

Music by Claude-Michel Schönberg
Lyrics by Alain Boublil,
Jean-Marc Natel and Herbert Kretzmer

Moderately slow

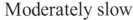

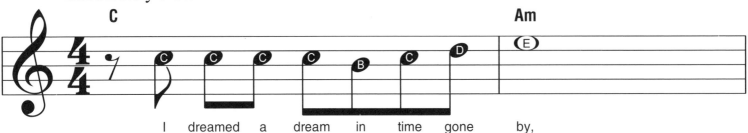

I dreamed a dream in time gone by,

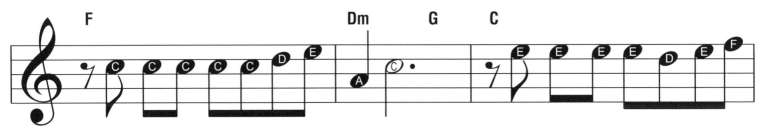

when hope was high and life worth liv - ing. I dreamed that love would nev - er

die. I dreamed that God would be for - giv - ing.

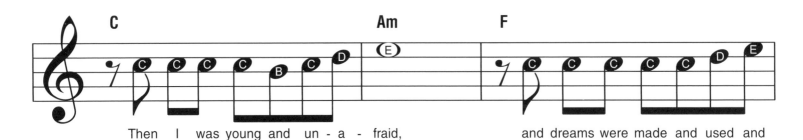

Then I was young and un - a - fraid, and dreams were made and used and

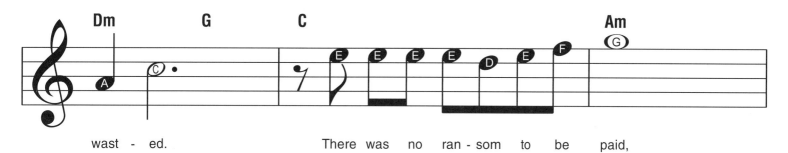

wast - ed.   There was no ran - som to be paid,

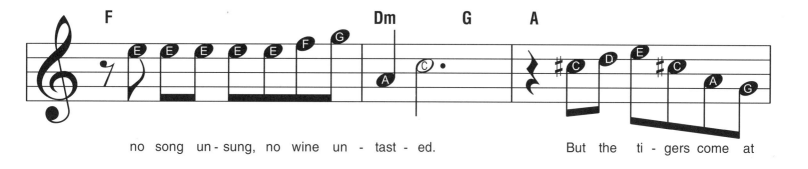

no song un - sung, no wine un - tast - ed.   But the ti - gers come at

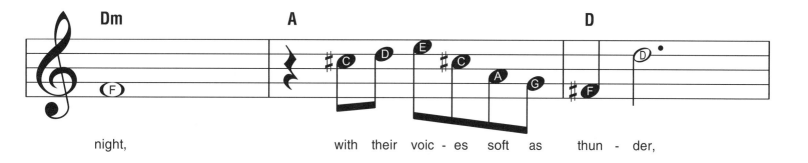

night,   with their voic - es soft as thun - der,

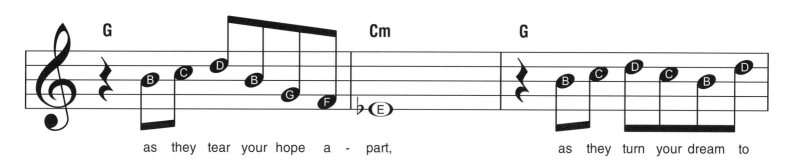

as they tear your hope a - part,   as they turn your dream to

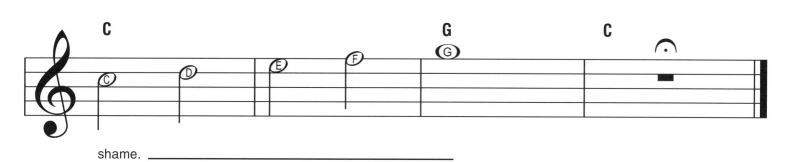

shame. _____

I Will Remember You
Theme from THE BROTHERS McMULLEN

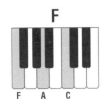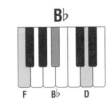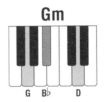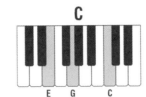

Words and Music by Sarah McLachlan,
Seamus Egan and Dave Merenda

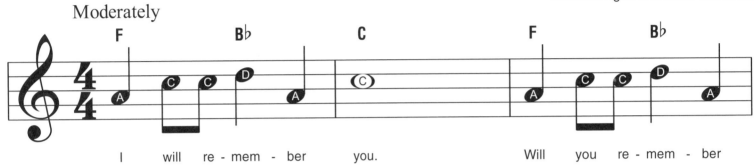

I will re-mem-ber you. Will you re-mem-ber

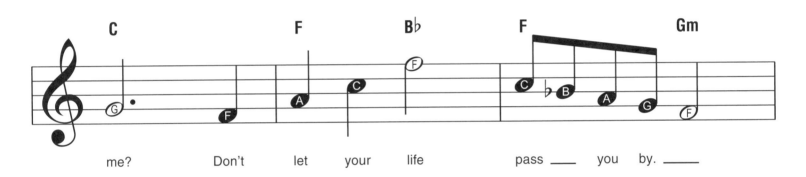

me? Don't let your life pass ___ you by. ___

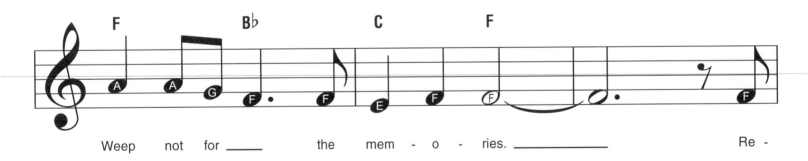

Weep not for ___ the mem-o-ries. ___ Re-

mem-ber the good times that we had. ___ We let them slip a-way from us when

37

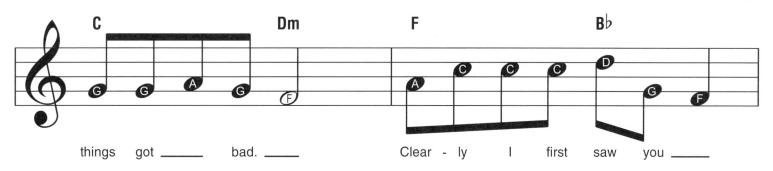

things got _____ bad. _____ Clear - ly I first saw you _____

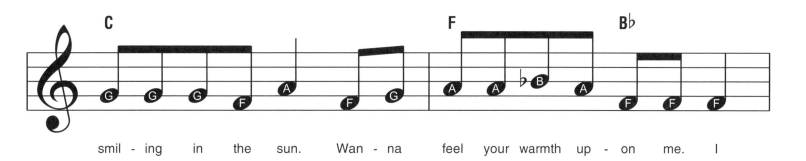

smil - ing in the sun. Wan - na feel your warmth up - on me. I

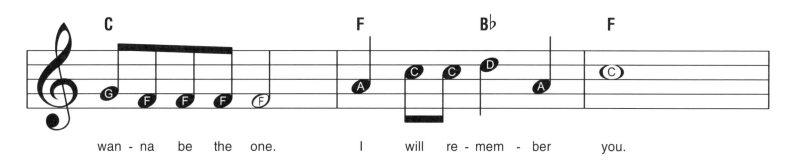

wan - na be the one. I will re - mem - ber you.

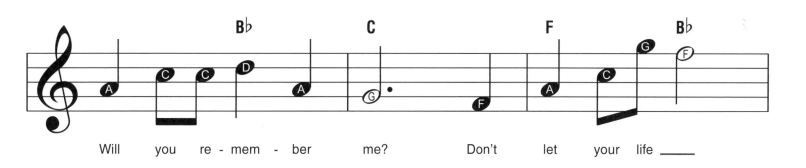

Will you re - mem - ber me? Don't let your life _____

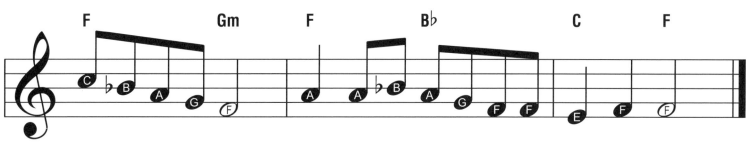

pass ___ you by. ___ Weep not for _____ the mem - o - ries.

It Is Well with My Soul

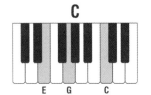
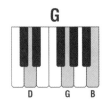
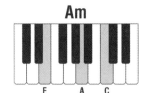
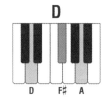
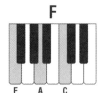

Words by Horatio G. Spafford
Music by Philip P. Bliss

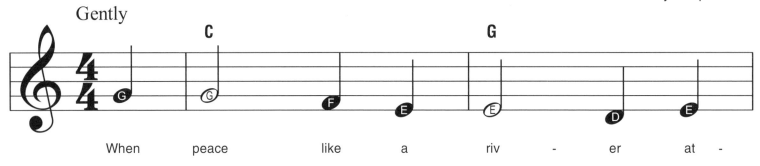

When peace like a riv - er at -

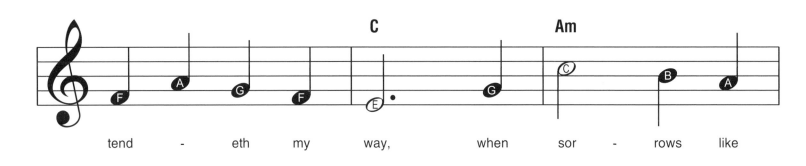

tend - eth my way, when sor - rows like

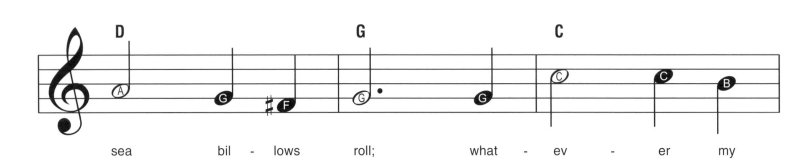

sea bil - lows roll; what - ev - er my

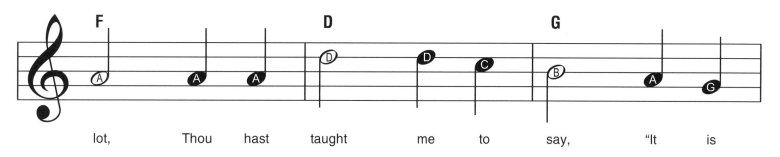

lot, Thou hast taught me to say, "It is

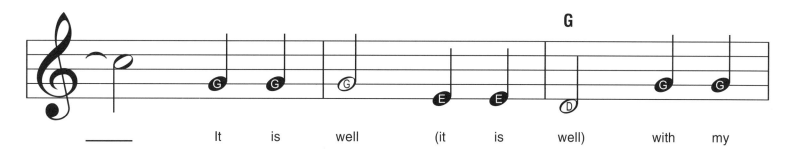

well, it is well with my soul." _____

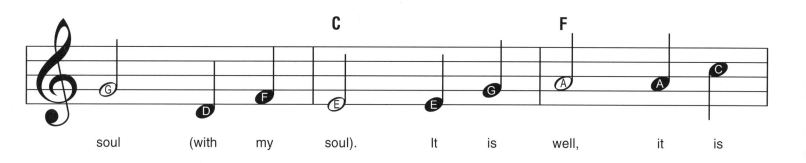

_____ It is well (it is well) with my

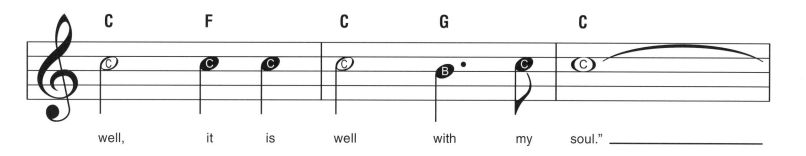

soul (with my soul). It is well, it is

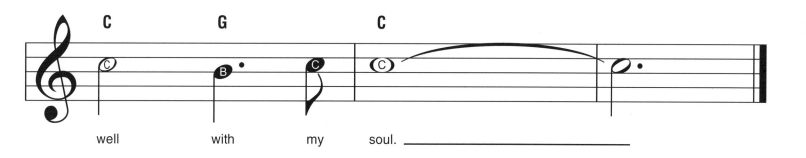

well with my soul. _____

Longer

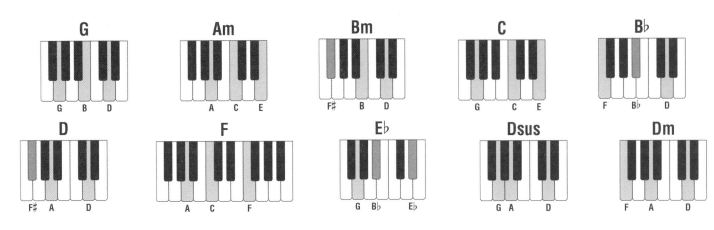

Words and Music by
Dan Fogelberg

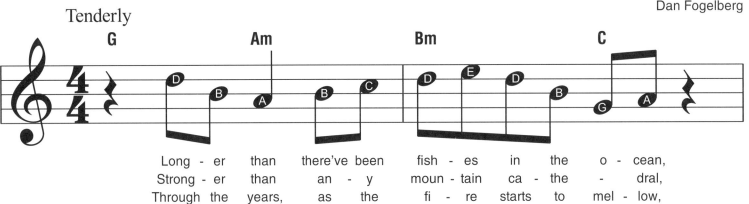

Long - er than there've been fish - es in the o - cean,
Strong - er than an - y moun - tain ca - the - - dral,
Through the years, as the fi - re starts to mel - low,

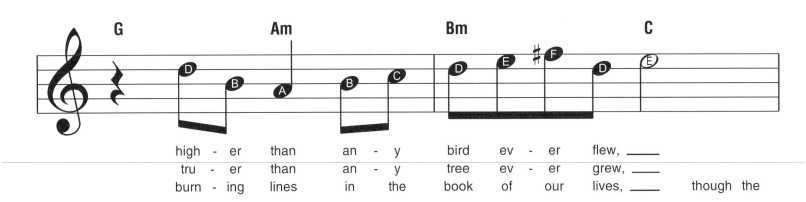

high - er than an - y bird ev - er flew, _____
tru - er than an - y tree ev - er grew, _____
burn - ing lines in the book of our lives, _____ though the

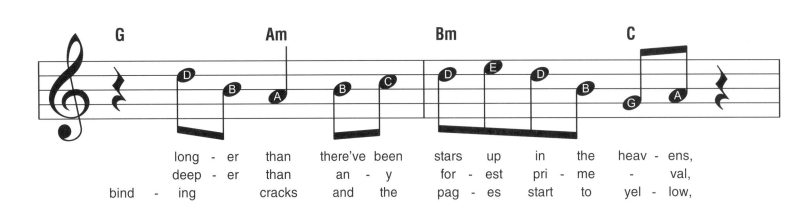

long - er than there've been stars up in the heav - ens,
deep - er than an - y for - est pri - me - val,
bind - ing cracks and the pag - es start to yel - low,

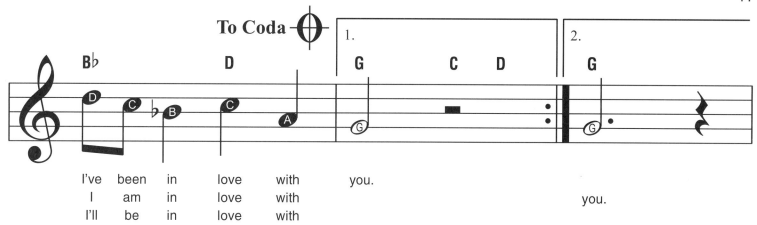

I've been in love with you.
I am in love with you.
I'll be in love with

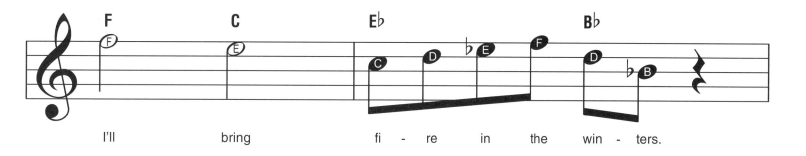

I'll bring fi - re in the win - ters.

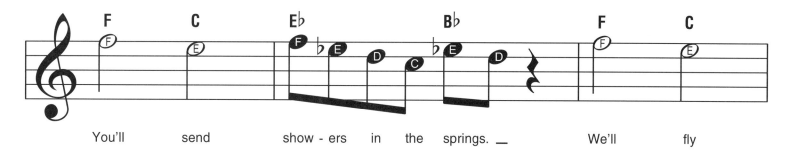

You'll send show - ers in the springs. __ We'll fly

D.C. al Coda
(Return to beginning,
play to ⊕ and skip to Coda)

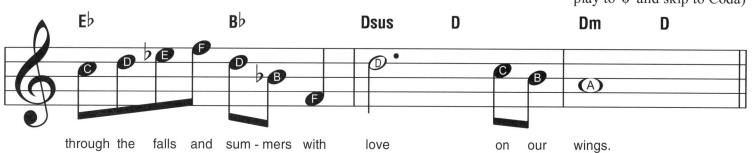

through the falls and sum - mers with love on our wings.

CODA

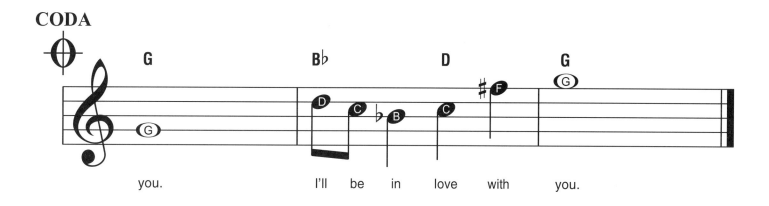

you. I'll be in love with you.

Lovely

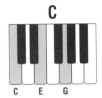
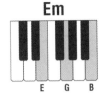
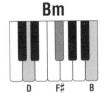

Words and Music by Billie Eilish O'Connell,
Finneas O'Connell and Khalid Robinson

Moderate Ballad

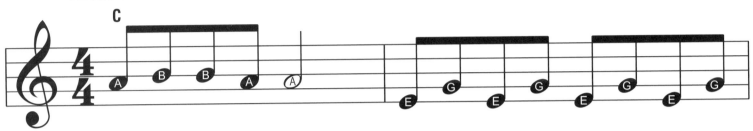

Thought I found a way, *(Instrumental)*

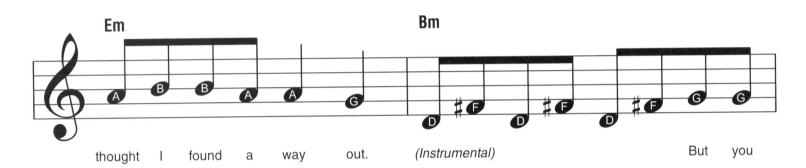

thought I found a way out. *(Instrumental)* But you

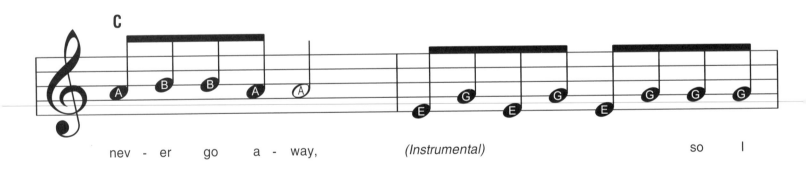

nev- er go a- way, *(Instrumental)* so I

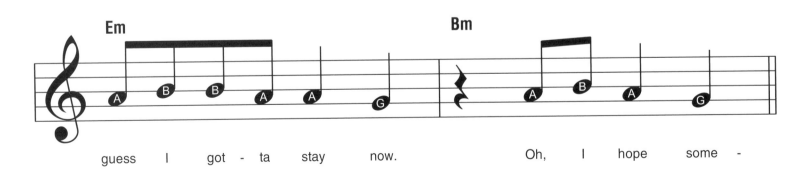

guess I got- ta stay now. Oh, I hope some-

43

Lullaby

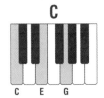
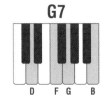
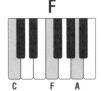

By Johannes Brahms

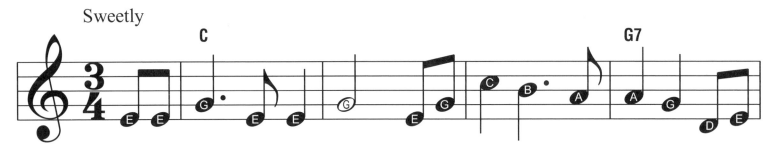

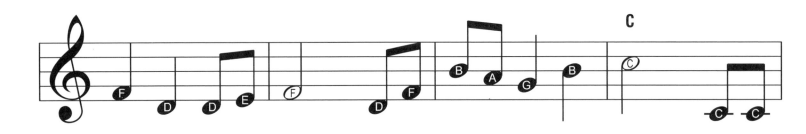

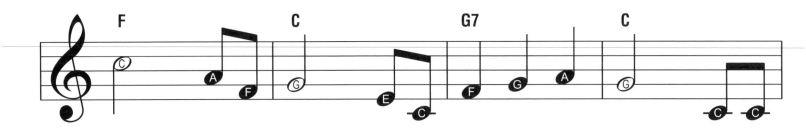

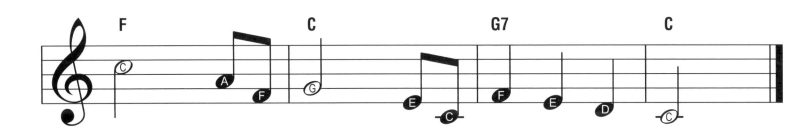

The Music of the Night
from THE PHANTOM OF THE OPERA

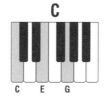

Music by Andrew Lloyd Webber
Lyrics by Charles Hart
Additional Lyrics by Richard Stilgoe

Slowly, with much expression

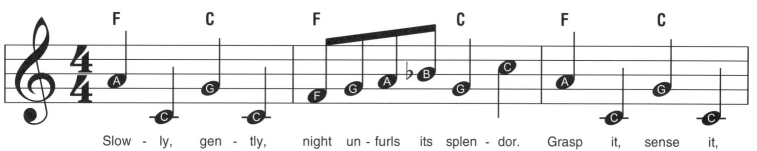

Slow - ly, gen - tly, night un - furls its splen - dor. Grasp it, sense it,

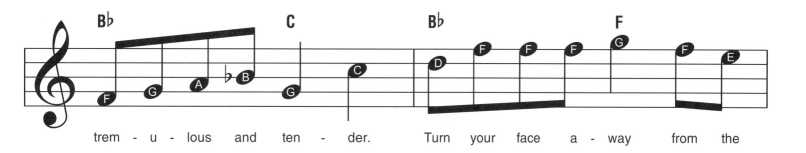

trem - u - lous and ten - der. Turn your face a - way from the

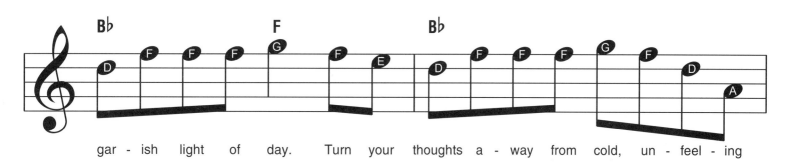

gar - ish light of day. Turn your thoughts a - way from cold, un - feel - ing

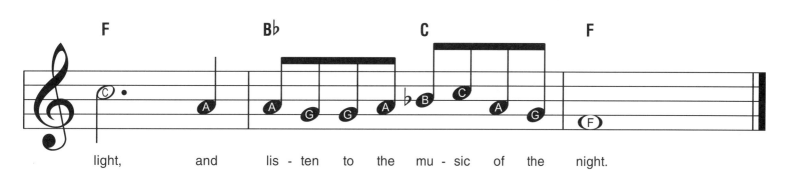

light, and lis - ten to the mu - sic of the night.

Lullabye
(Goodnight, My Angel)

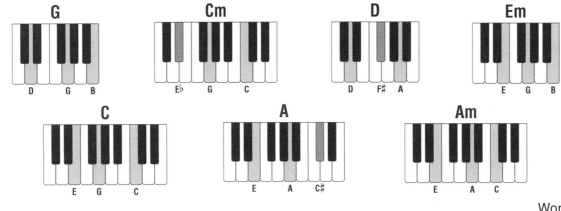

Words and Music by
Billy Joel

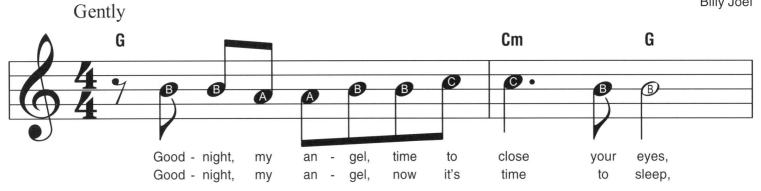

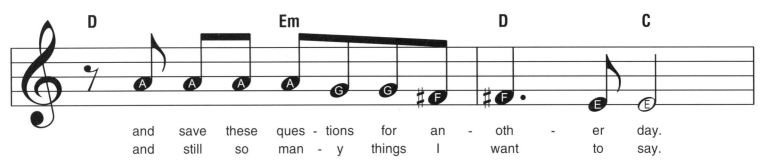

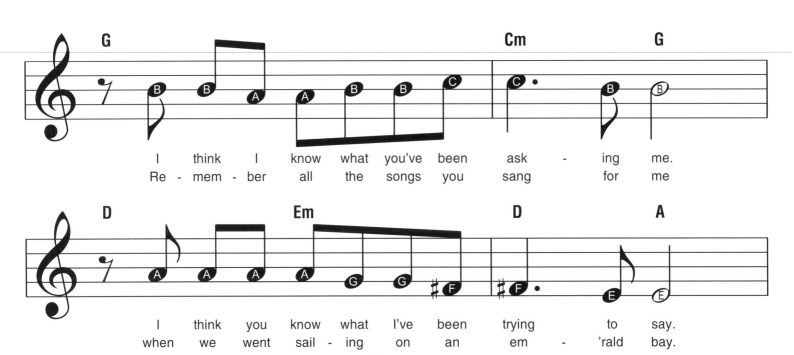

Meditation
from THAÏS

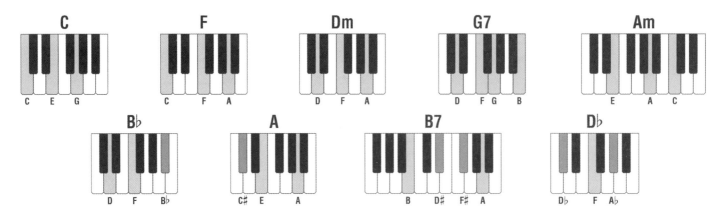

By Jules Massenet

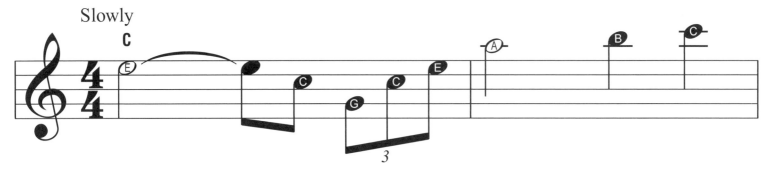

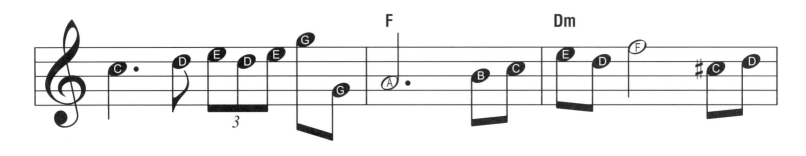

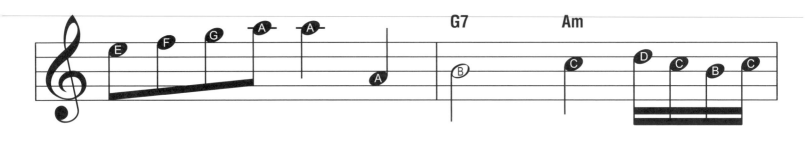

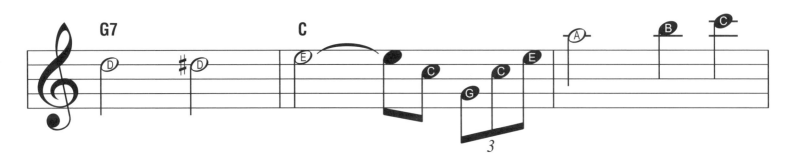

Memory
from CATS

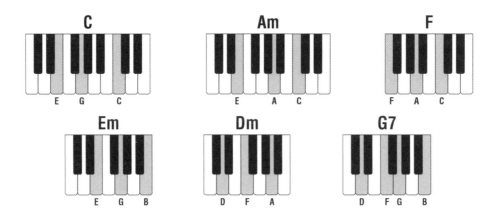

Music by Andrew Lloyd Webber
Text by Trevor Nunn after T.S. Eliot

Flowing

Mid - night, _____ not a sound from the
Mem - 'ry, _____ all a - lone in the

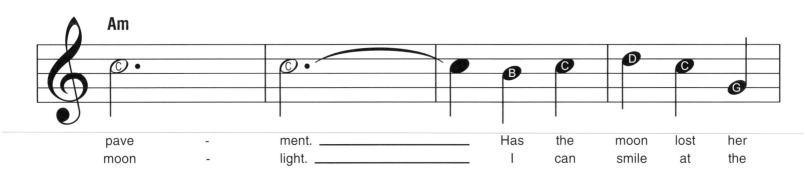

pave - ment. _____ Has the moon lost her
moon - light. _____ I can smile at the

mem - 'ry? _____ She is smil - ing a -
old days, _____ I was beau - ti - ful

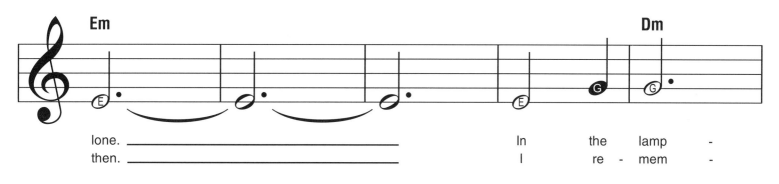

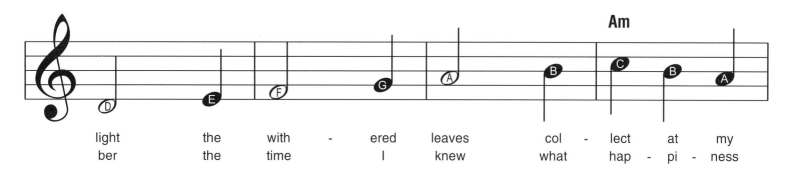

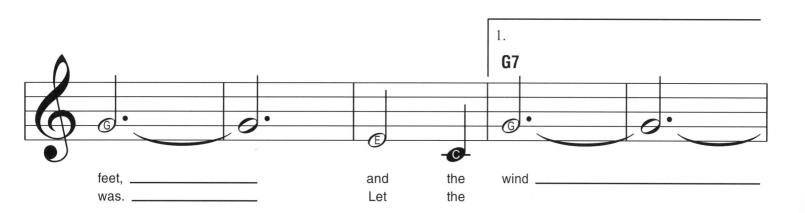

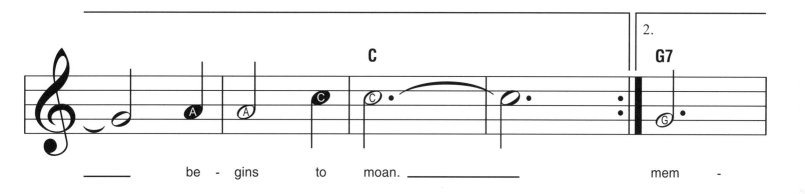

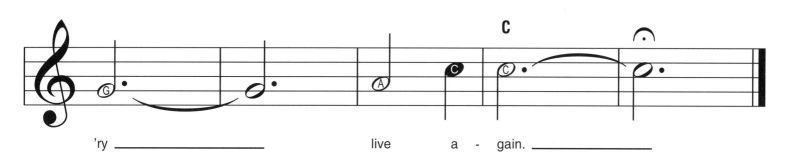

Misty

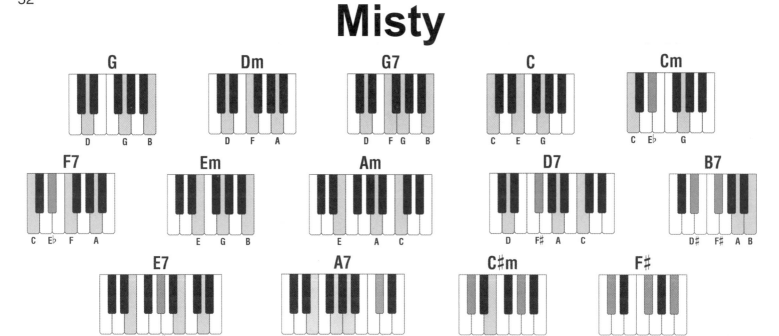

Words by Johnny Burke
Music by Erroll Garner

53

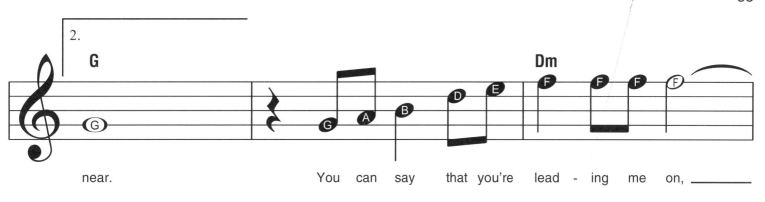

near.　You can say that you're lead-ing me on,

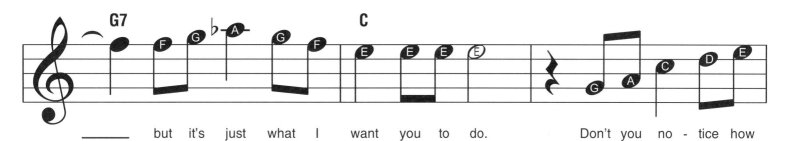

but it's just what I want you to do.　Don't you no-tice how

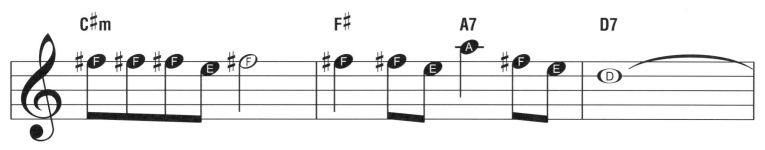

hope-less-ly I'm lost?　That's why I'm fol-low-ing you.

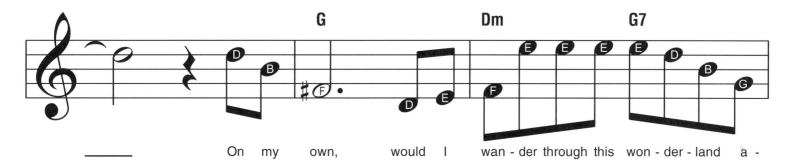

On my own, would I wan-der through this won-der-land a-

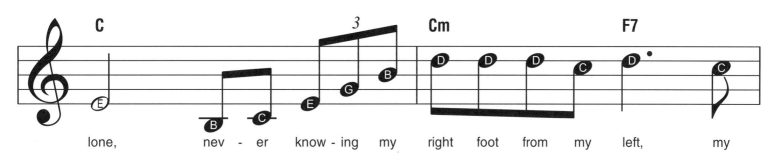

lone, nev-er know-ing my right foot from my left, my

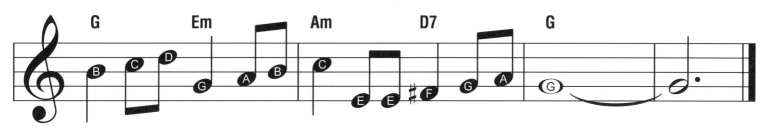

hat from my glove? I'm too mist-y and too much in love.

Moon River
from the Paramount Picture BREAKFAST AT TIFFANY'S

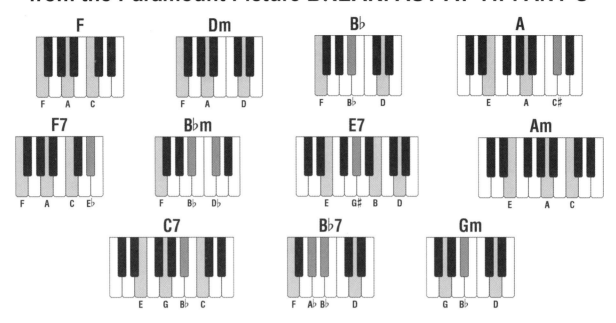

Words by Johnny Mercer
Music by Henry Mancini

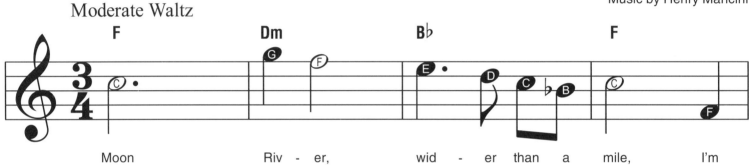

Moon Riv - er, wid - er than a mile, I'm

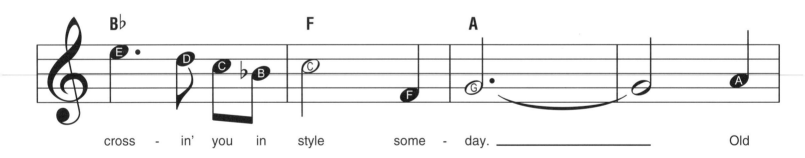

cross - in' you in style some - day. _____ Old

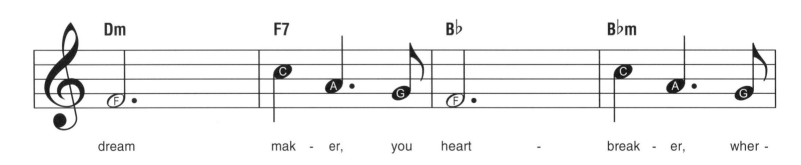

dream mak - er, you heart - break - er, wher -

Morning Has Broken

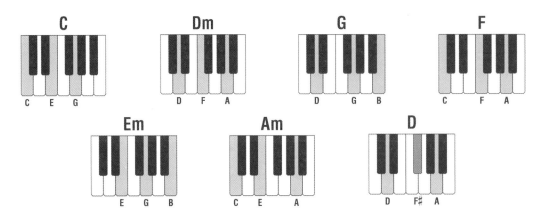

Words by Eleanor Farjeon
Music by Cat Stevens

Flowing
(no chord)

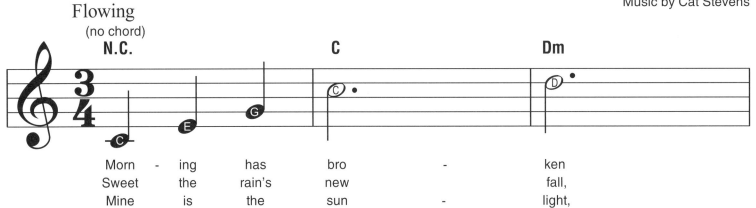

Morn - ing   has   bro   -   ken
Sweet   the   rain's new   fall,
Mine   is   the   sun   -   light,

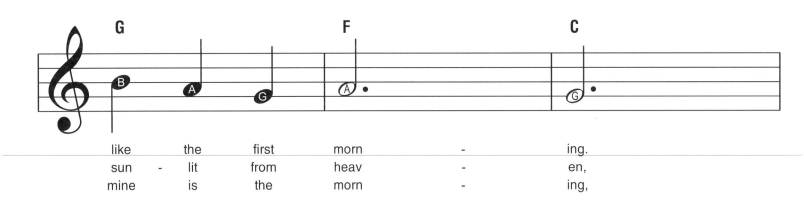

like   the   first   morn   -   ing.
sun - lit   from   heav   -   en,
mine   is   the   morn   -   ing,

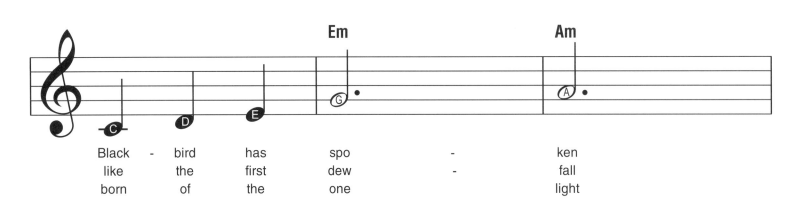

Black - bird   has   spo   -   ken
like   the   first   dew   -   fall
born   of   the   one   light

My Heart Will Go On
(Love Theme from 'Titanic')
from the Paramount and Twentieth Century Fox Motion Picture TITANIC

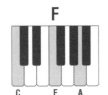
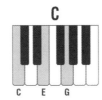
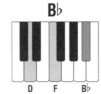

Music by James Horner
Lyric by Will Jennings

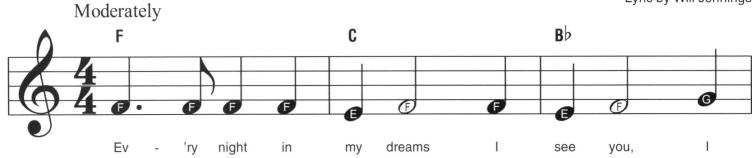

Ev - 'ry night in my dreams I see you, I

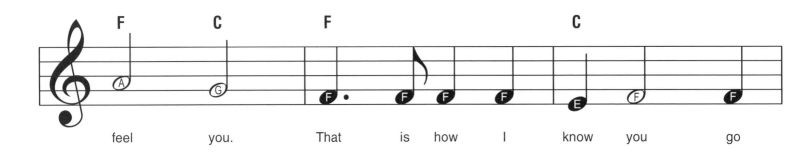

feel you. That is how I know you go

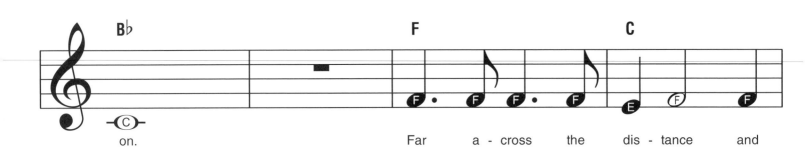

on. Far a-cross the dis- tance and

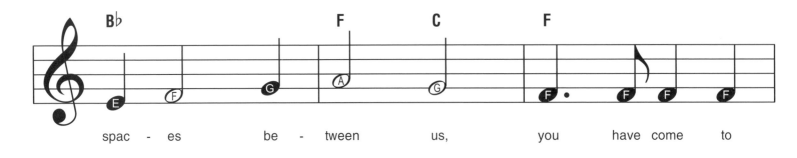

spac - es be - tween us, you have come to

Near to the Heart of God

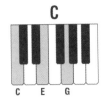

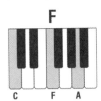

Words and Music by
Cleland B. McAfee

Pie Jesu

from REQUIEM

By Andrew Lloyd Webber

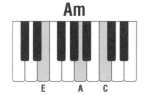 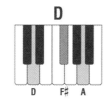 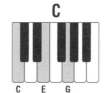 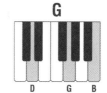 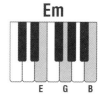

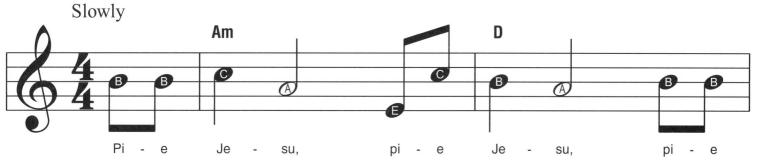

Pi – e Je – su, pi – e Je – su, pi – e

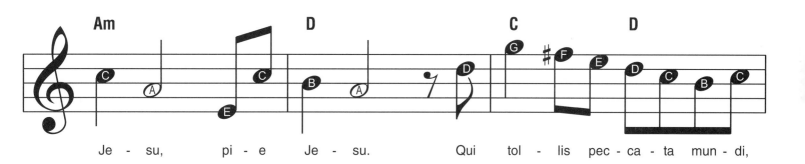

Je – su, pi – e Je – su. Qui tol – lis pec – ca – ta mun – di,

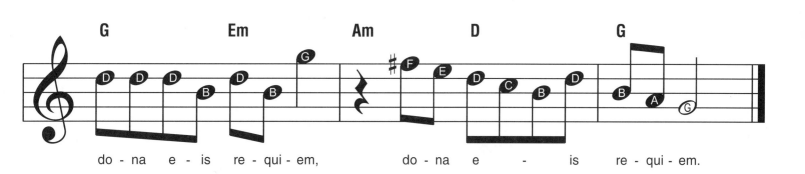

do – na e – is re – qui – em, do – na e – is re – qui – em.

'O Sole Mio

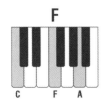
F

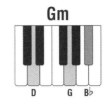
Gm

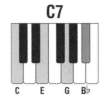
C7

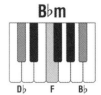
B♭m

Words by Giovanni Capurro
Music by Eduardo di Capua

Moderately

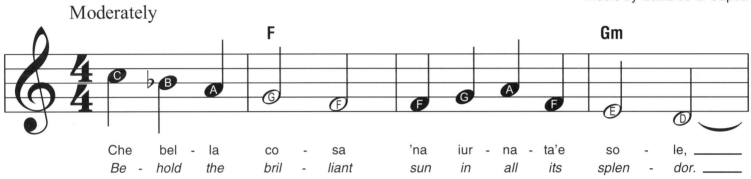

Che bel - la co - sa 'na iur - na - ta'e so - le, _____
Be - hold the bril - liant sun in all its splen - dor. _____

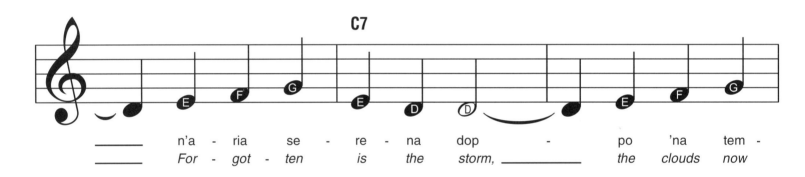

_____ n'a - ria se - re - na dop - po 'na tem -
_____ For - got - ten is the storm, _____ the clouds now

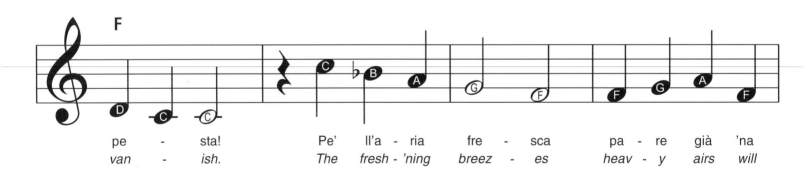

pe - sta! Pe' ll'a - ria fre - sca pa - re già 'na
van - ish. The fresh - 'ning breez - es heav - y airs will

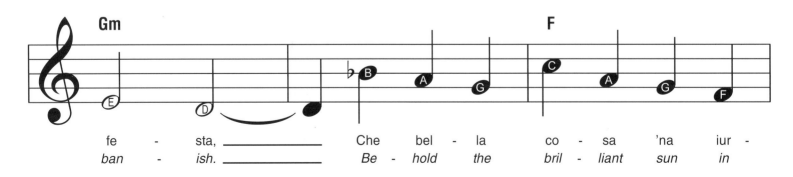

fe - sta, _____ Che bel - la co - sa 'na iur -
ban - ish. _____ Be - hold the bril - liant sun in

63

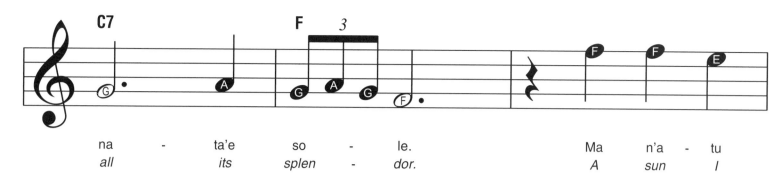

na - ta'e so - le.
all its splen - dor.
Ma n'a - tu

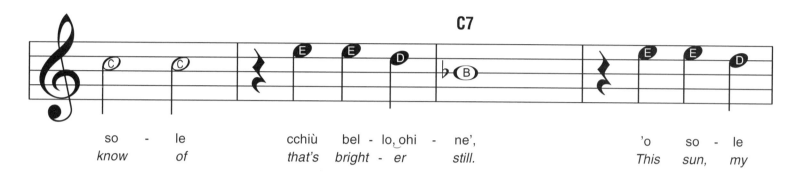

so - le cchiù bel - lo, ohi - ne', 'o so - le
know of that's bright - er still. This sun, my

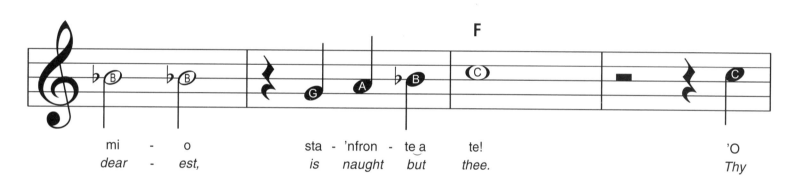

mi - o sta - 'nfron - te a te! 'O
dear - est, is naught but thee. Thy

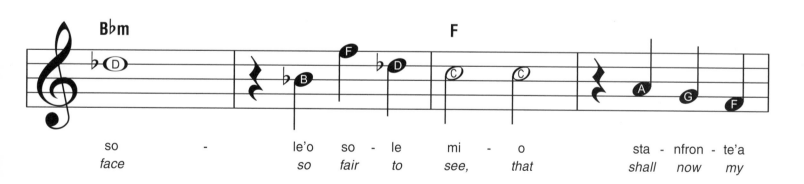

so - le 'o so - le mi - o sta - nfron - te a
face so fair to see, that shall now my

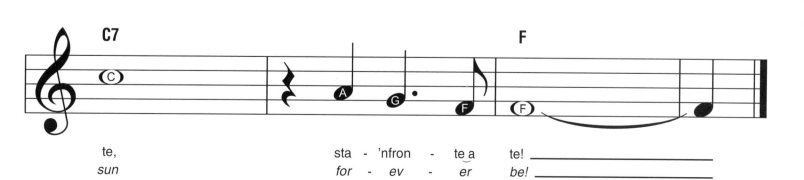

te, sta - 'nfron - te a te! _____
sun for - ev - er be! _____

Over the Rainbow

from THE WIZARD OF OZ

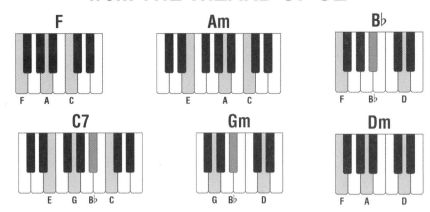

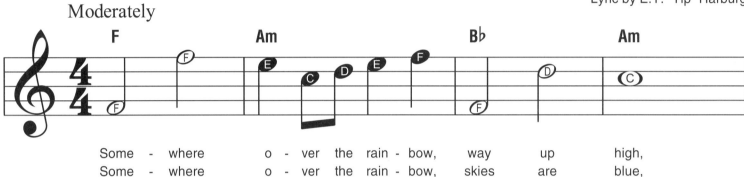

Music by Harold Arlen
Lyric by E.Y. "Yip" Harburg

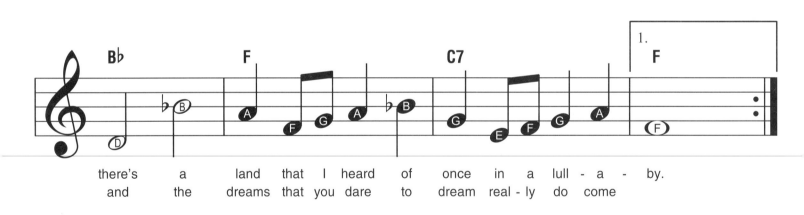

Some - where o - ver the rain - bow, way up high,
Some - where o - ver the rain - bow, skies are blue,

there's a land that I heard of once in a lull - a - by.
and the dreams that you dare to dream real - ly do come

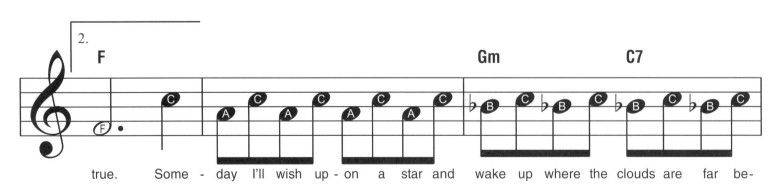

true. Some - day I'll wish up - on a star and wake up where the clouds are far be-

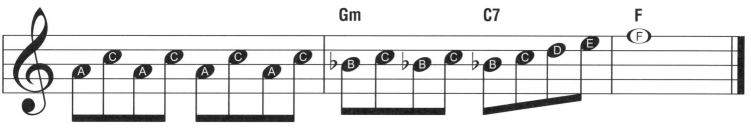

Perfect

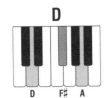
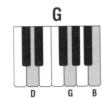
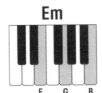
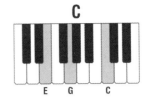

Words and Music by
Ed Sheeran

Moderately slow, in 2

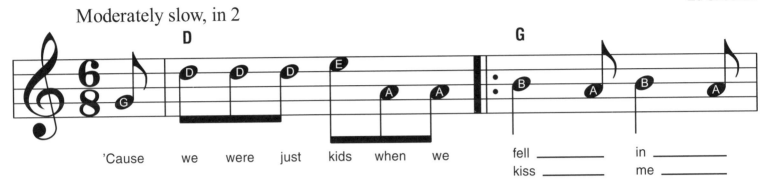

'Cause we were just kids when we fell _____ in _____
kiss _____ me _____

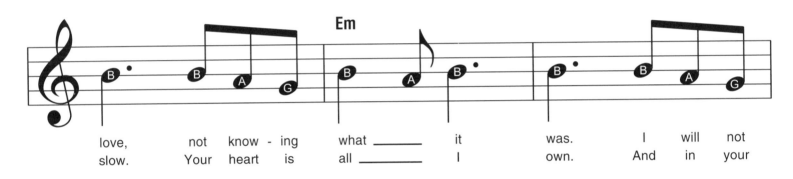

love, not know - ing what _____ it was. I will not
slow. Your heart is all _____ I own. And in your

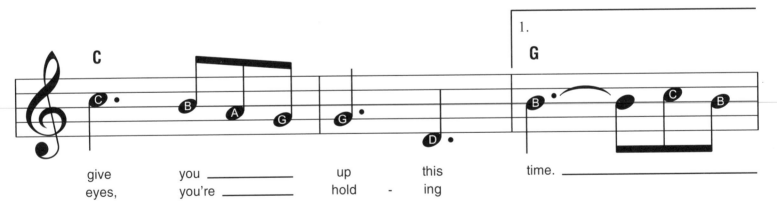

give you _____ up this time. _____
eyes, you're _____ hold - ing

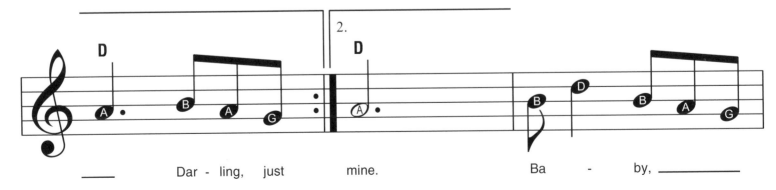

____ Dar - ling, just mine. Ba - by, _____

Princess Leia's Theme

from STAR WARS: A NEW HOPE

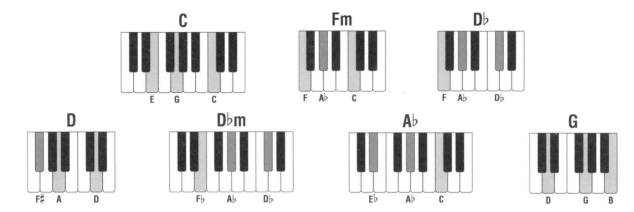

Music by
John Williams

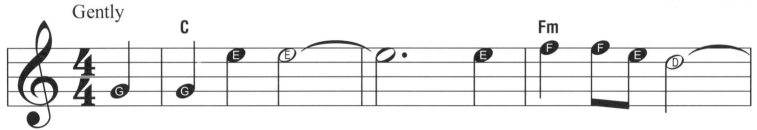

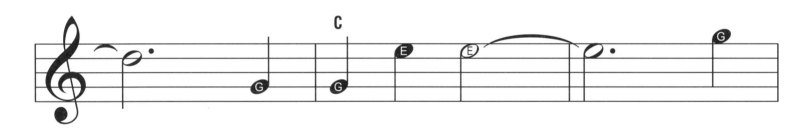

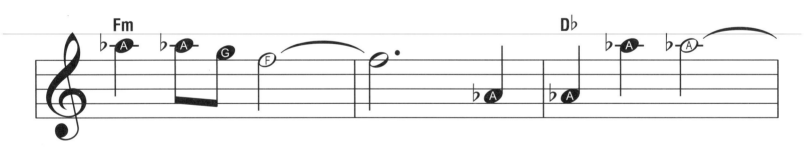

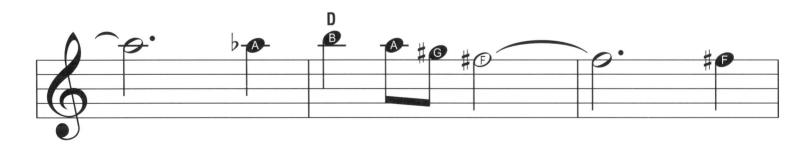

The Rainbow Connection
from THE MUPPET MOVIE

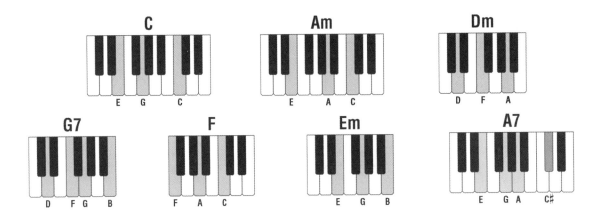

Words and Music by Paul Williams
and Kenneth L. Ascher

Moderately

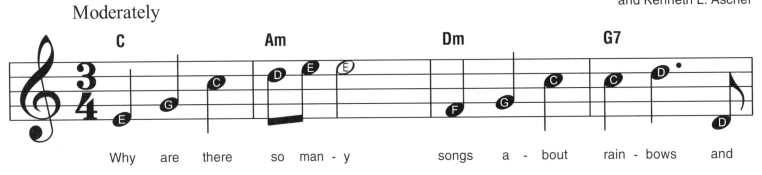

Why are there so man-y songs a - bout rain - bows and

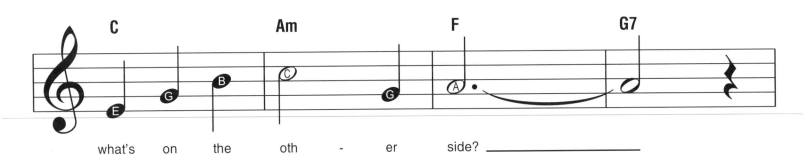

what's on the oth - er side? _____

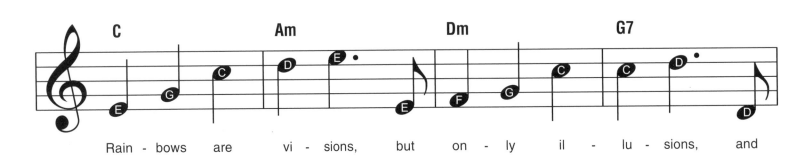

Rain - bows are vi - sions, but on - ly il - lu - sions, and

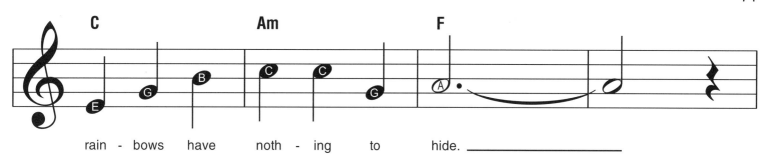

rain - bows have noth - ing to hide. _____

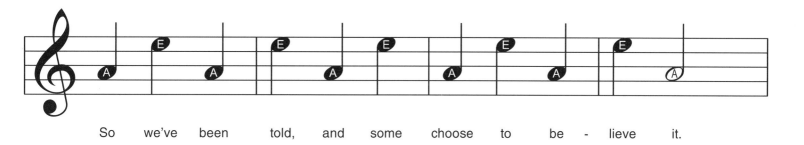

So we've been told, and some choose to be - lieve it.

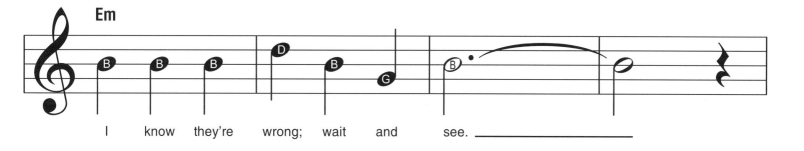

I know they're wrong; wait and see. _____

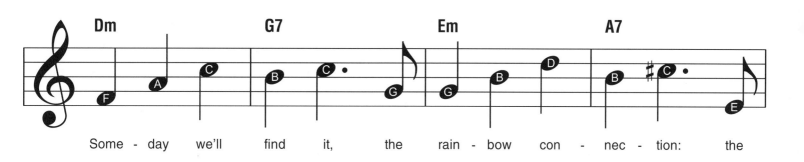

Some - day we'll find it, the rain - bow con - nec - tion: the

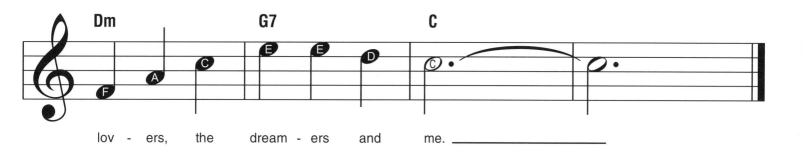

lov - ers, the dream - ers and me. _____

Savior, Like a Shepherd Lead Us

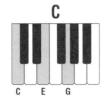
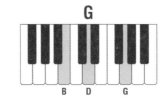

Words from *Hymns For The Young*
Attributed to Dorothy A. Thrupp
Music by William B. Bradbury

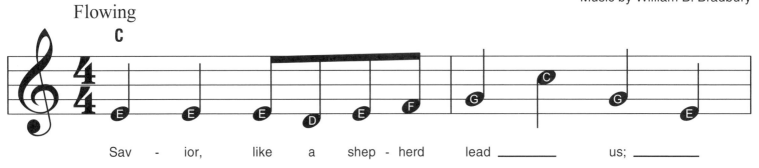

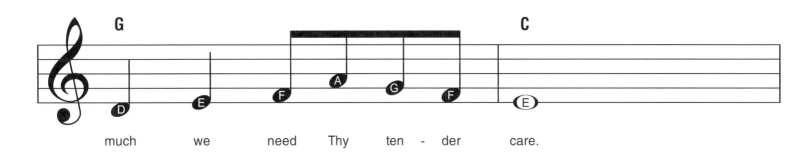

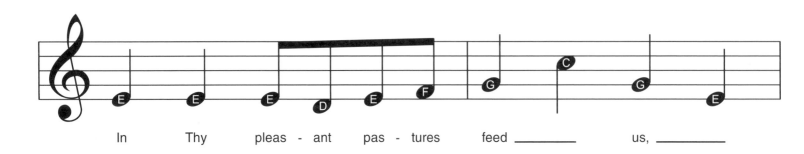

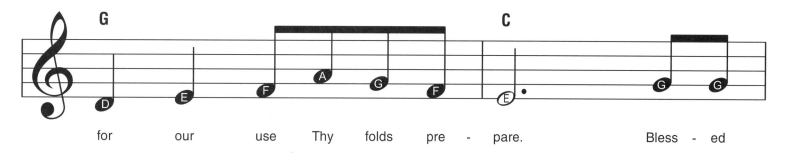

for our use Thy folds pre - pare. Bless - ed

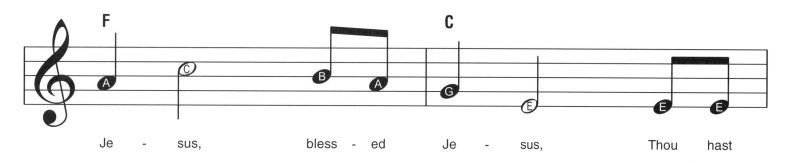

Je - sus, bless - ed Je - sus, Thou hast

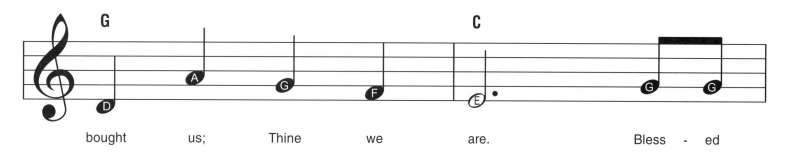

bought us; Thine we are. Bless - ed

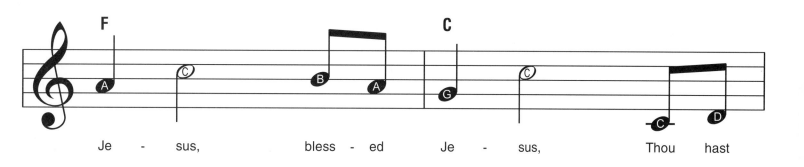

Je - sus, bless - ed Je - sus, Thou hast

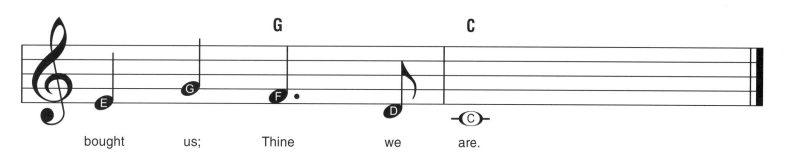

bought us; Thine we are.

Send in the Clowns
from A LITTLE NIGHT MUSIC

Words and Music by
Stephen Sondheim

Slowly, with expression

Is - n't it   rich?
bliss?

Are we a   pair?
Don't you ap - prove?

Me here at
One who keeps

last on the ground,
tear - ing a - round,

you in mid - air.
one who can't move.

Send in the   clowns. _____
Where are the

_____

Is - n't it   clowns?

Send in the clowns.

Just when I'd

She's Got a Way

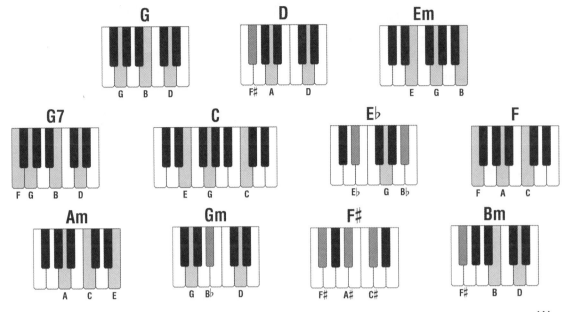

Words and Music by
Billy Joel

Slowly

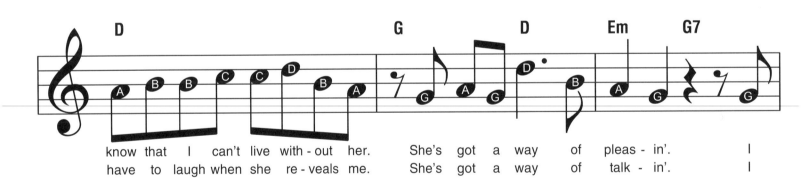

She's got a way a - bout her. I don't know what it is, but I
She's got a smile that heals me. I don't know why it is, but I

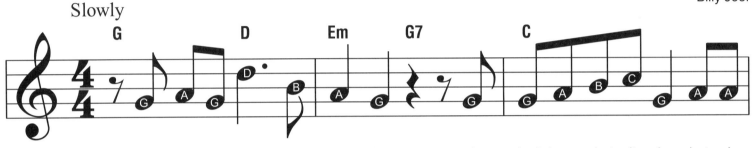

know that I can't live with - out her. She's got a way of pleas - in'. I
have to laugh when she re - veals me. She's got a way of talk - in'. I

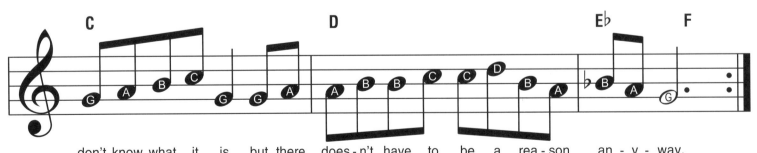

don't know what it is, but there does - n't have to be a rea - son an - y - way.
don't know why it is, but it lifts me up when we are walk - in' an - y - where.

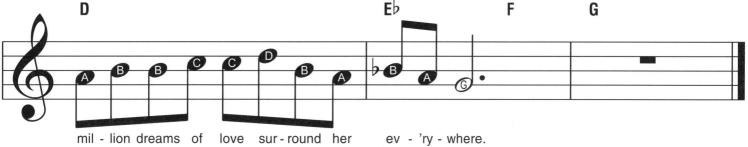

Shenandoah

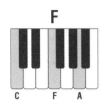
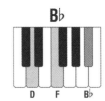
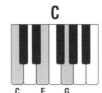
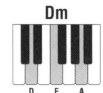
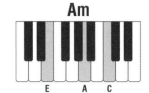

American Folksong

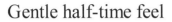

Gentle half-time feel

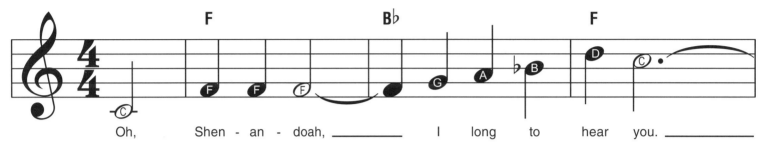

Oh, Shen - an - doah, _____ I long to hear you. _____

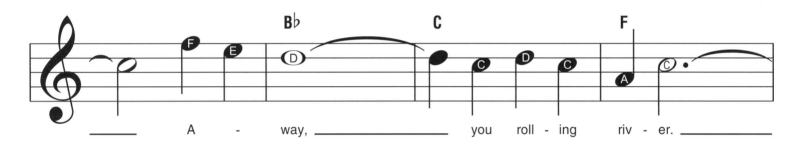

_____ A - way, _____ you roll - ing riv - er. _____

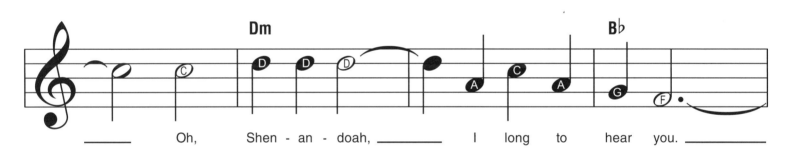

_____ Oh, Shen - an - doah, _____ I long to hear you. _____

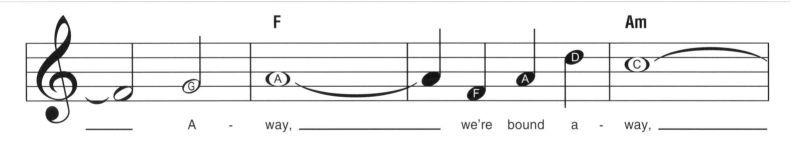

_____ A - way, _____ we're bound a - way, _____

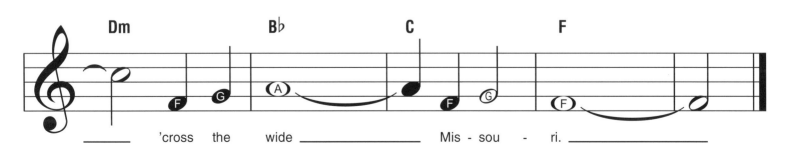

_____ 'cross the wide _____ Mis - sou - ri. _____

Water Is Wide

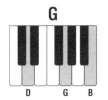
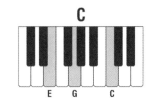
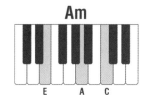
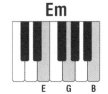
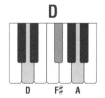

Traditional

Gently
(no chord)

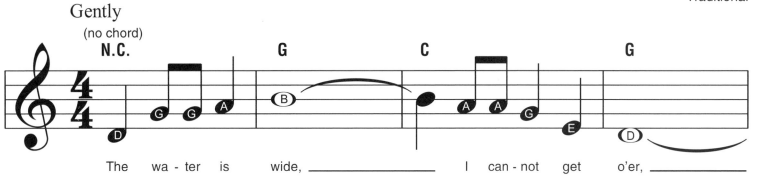

The wa-ter is wide, _____ I can-not get o'er, _____

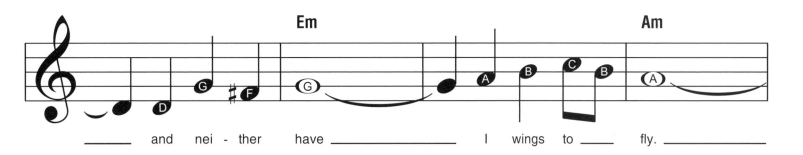

_____ and nei-ther have _____ I wings to ____ fly. _____

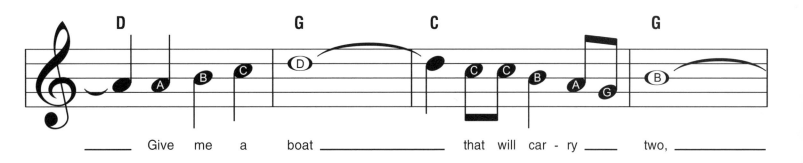

_____ Give me a boat _____ that will car-ry ____ two, _____

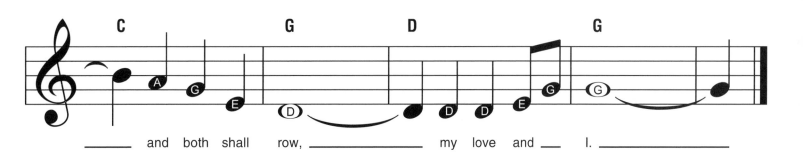

_____ and both shall row, _____ my love and ___ I. _____

Someone to Watch Over Me

from OH, KAY!

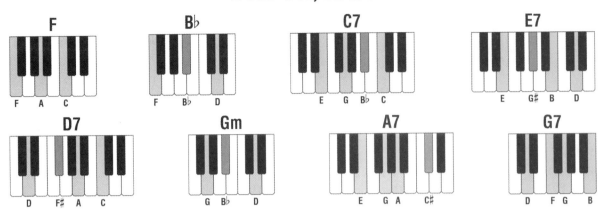

Music and Lyrics by George Gershwin
and Ira Gershwin

Moderately slow Shuffle

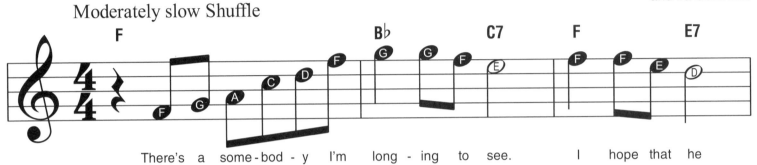

There's a some-bod-y I'm long-ing to see. I hope that he

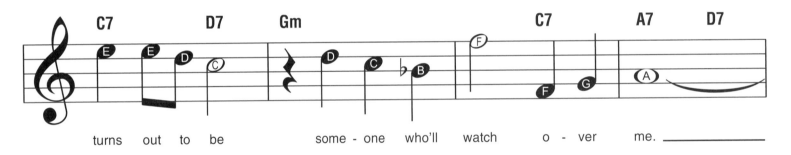

turns out to be some-one who'll watch o-ver me.

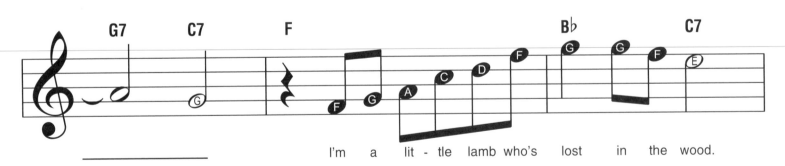

I'm a lit-tle lamb who's lost in the wood.

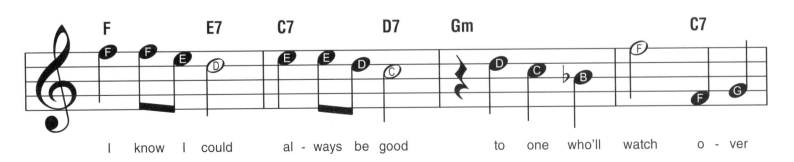

I know I could al-ways be good to one who'll watch o-ver

81

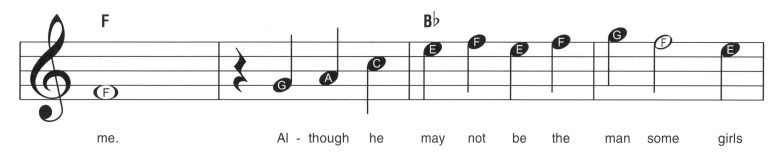

me.   Al - though he may not be the man some girls

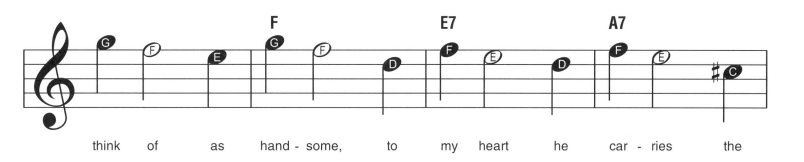

think of as hand - some, to my heart he car - ries the

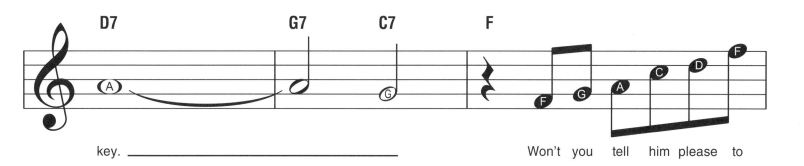

key. _____ Won't you tell him please to

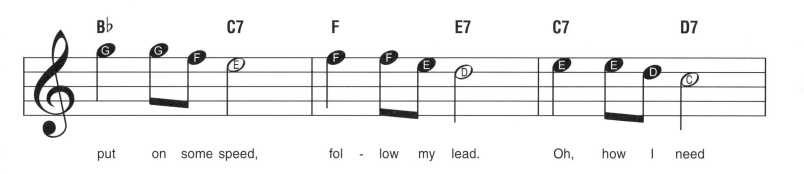

put on some speed, fol - low my lead. Oh, how I need

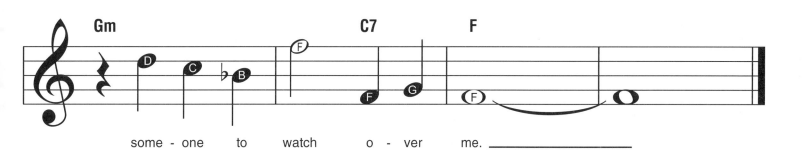

some - one to watch o - ver me. _____

Somewhere, My Love
Lara's Theme from DOCTOR ZHIVAGO

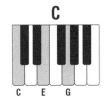

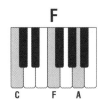

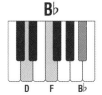

Lyric by Paul Francis Webster
Music by Maurice Jarre

Tenderly

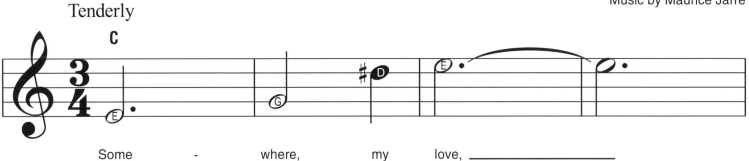

Some - where, my love, _____
Some - where a hill _____

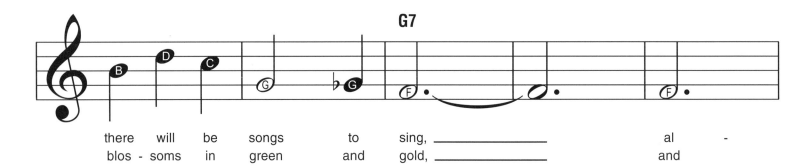

there will be songs to sing, _____ al -
blos - soms in green and gold, _____ and

though the snow _____ cov - ers the hope of
there are dreams, _____ all that your heart can

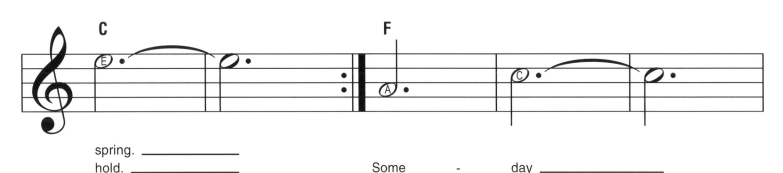

spring. _____
hold. _____ Some - day _____

Somewhere Out There

from AN AMERICAN TAIL

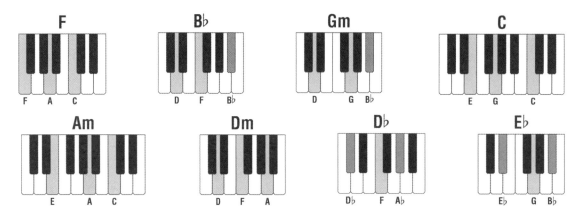

Music by Barry Mann and James Horner
Lyric by Cynthia Weil

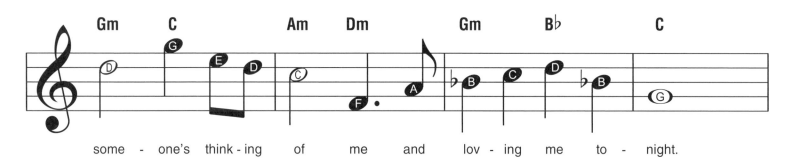

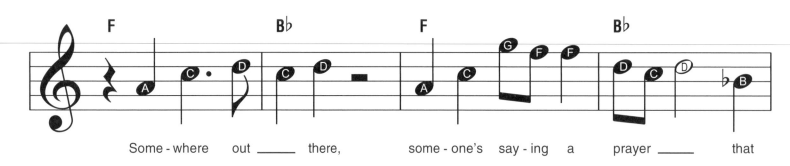

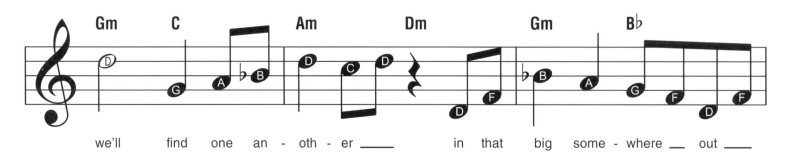

Song from a Secret Garden

By Rolf Lovland

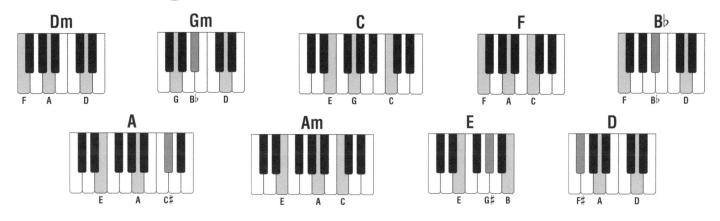

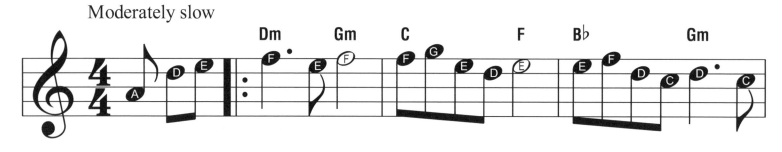

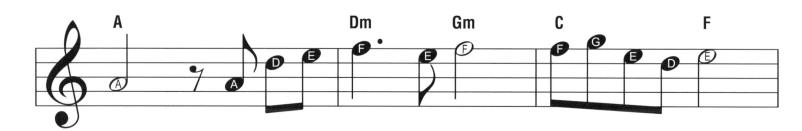

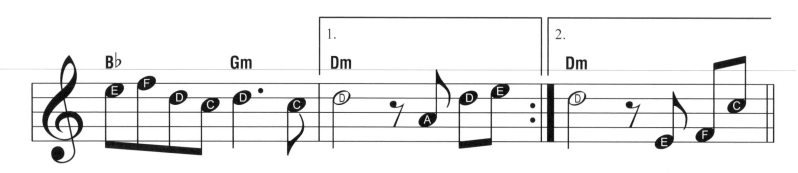

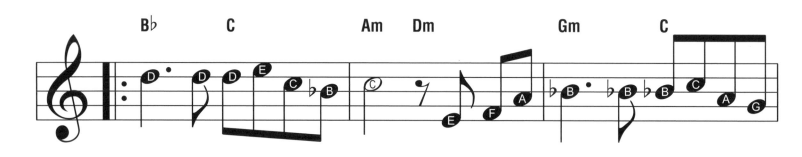

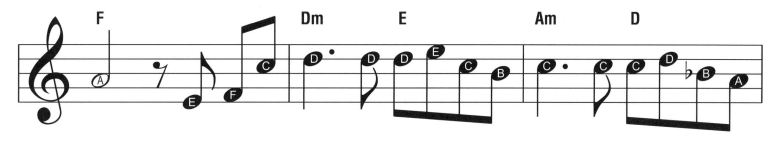

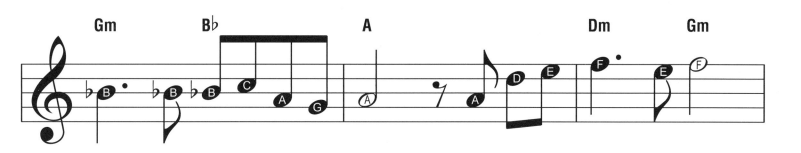

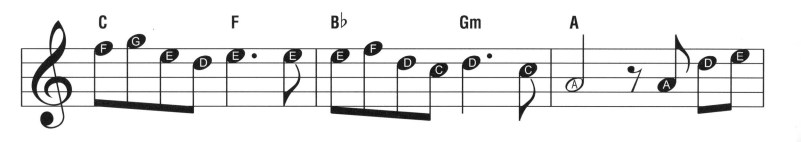

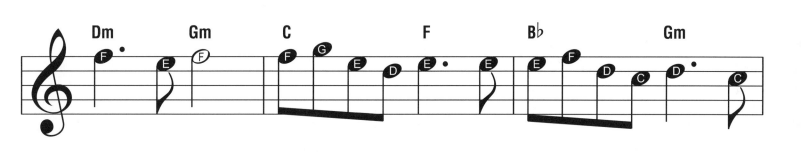

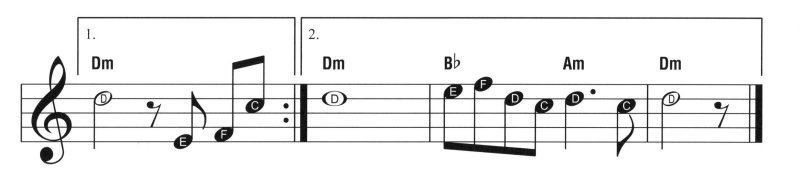

The Sound of Silence

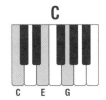
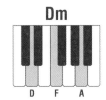
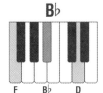
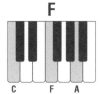

Words and Music by
Paul Simon

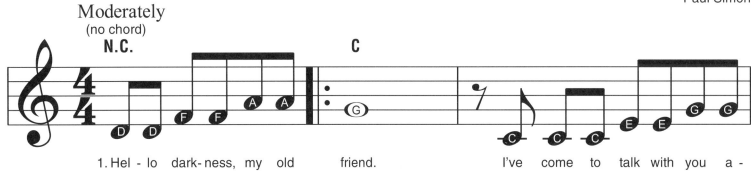

1. Hel - lo dark-ness, my old friend. I've come to talk with you a -
2.–5. *(See additional lyrics)*

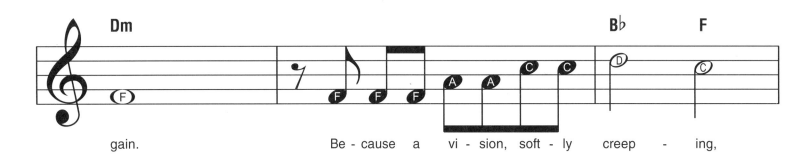

gain. Be - cause a vi - sion, soft - ly creep - ing,

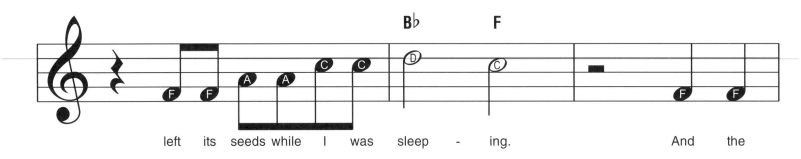

left its seeds while I was sleep - ing. And the

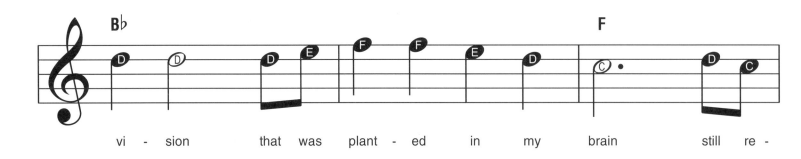

vi - sion that was plant - ed in my brain still re -

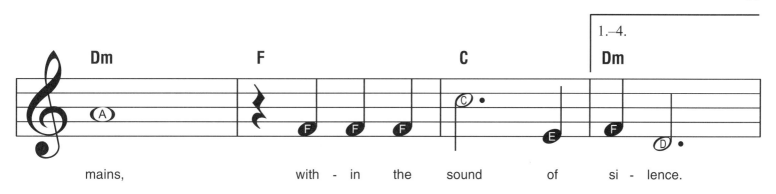

mains,   with - in   the   sound   of   si - lence.

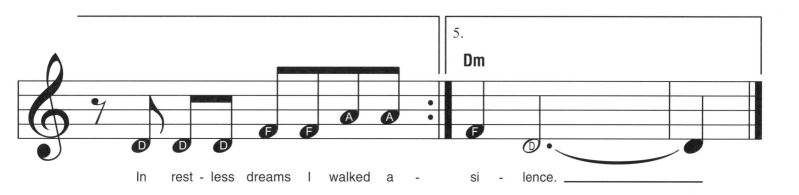

In   rest - less dreams I walked a -   si - lence. _____

Additional Lyrics

2. In restless dreams I walked alone,
   Narrow streets of cobblestone.
   'Neath the halo of a street lamp,
   I turned my collar to the cold and damp.
   When my eyes were stabbed by the flash of a neon light
   That split the night, and touched the sound of silence.

3. And in the naked light I saw
   Ten thousand people, maybe more.
   People talking without speaking,
   People hearing without listening,
   People writing songs that voices never share.
   And no one dare disturb the sound of silence.

4. "Fools!" said I, "You do not know
   Silence, like a cancer, grows.
   Hear my words that I might teach you,
   Take my arms that I might reach you."
   But my words, like silent raindrops fell,
   And echoed in the wells of silence.

5. And the people bowed and prayed
   To the neon god they made.
   And the sign flashed out its warning,
   In the words that it was forming.
   And the sign said, "The words of the prophets
   Are written on the subway walls and tenement halls,
   And whispered in the sounds of silence."

Think of Me
from THE PHANTOM OF THE OPERA

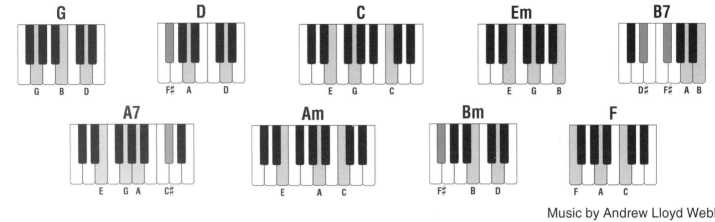

Music by Andrew Lloyd Webber
Lyrics by Charles Hart
Additional Lyrics by Richard Stilgoe

Moderately

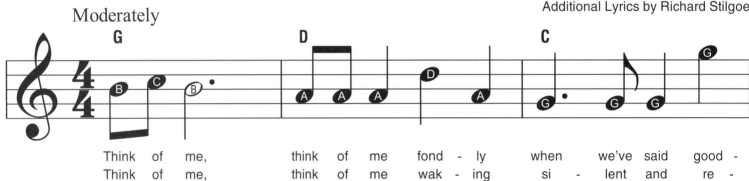

Think of me, think of me fond - ly when we've said good -
Think of me, think of me wak - ing si - lent and re -

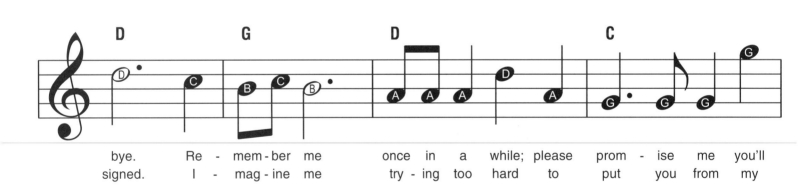

bye. Re - mem - ber me once in a while; please prom - ise me you'll
signed. I - mag - ine me try - ing too hard to put you from my

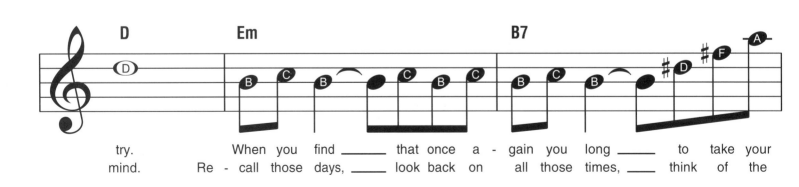

try. When you find _____ that once a - gain you long _____ to take your
mind. Re - call those days, _____ look back on all those times, _____ think of the

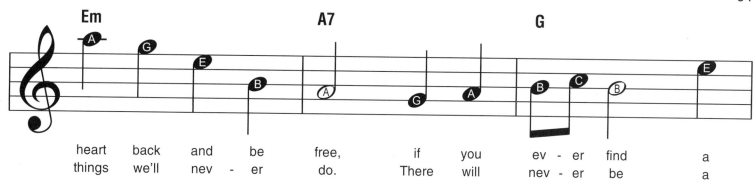

heart back and be free, if you ev - er find a a
things we'll nev - er do. There will nev - er be a a

To Coda

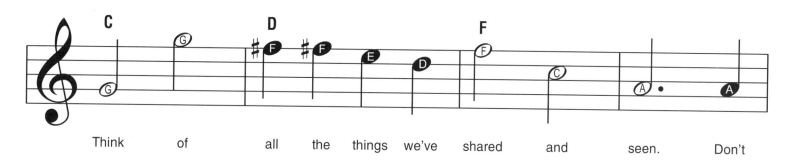

mo - ment, spare a thought for me.
day when I won't

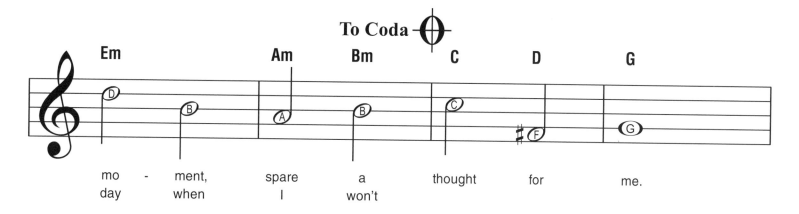

Think of all the things we've shared and seen. Don't

D.C. al Coda
(Return to beginning,
play to ✛ and skip to Coda)

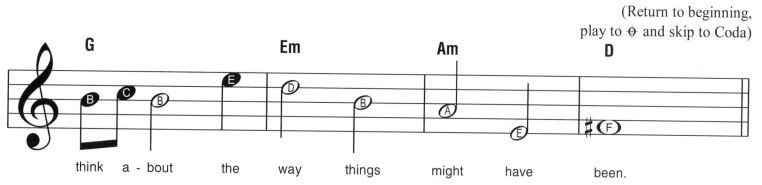

think a - bout the way things might have been.

CODA

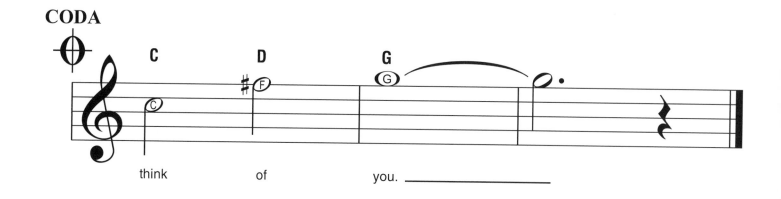

think of you. _____

A Thousand Years
from the Summit Entertainment film
THE TWILIGHT SAGA: BREAKING DAWN - Part 1

Words and Music by David Hodges
and Christina Perri

Till There Was You

from Meredith Willson's THE MUSIC MAN

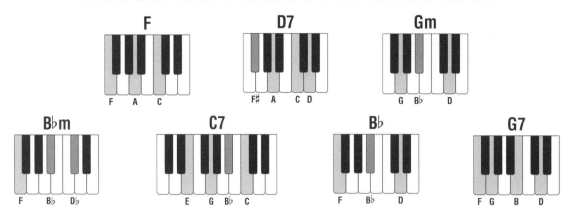

By Meredith Willson

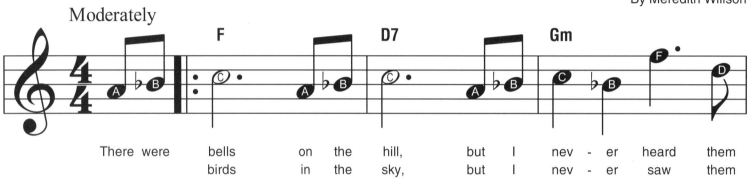

There were bells on the hill, but I nev - er heard them
birds in the sky, but I nev - er saw them

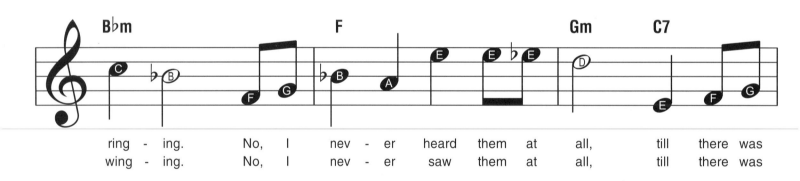

ring - ing. No, I nev - er heard them at all, till there was
wing - ing. No, I nev - er saw them at all, till there was

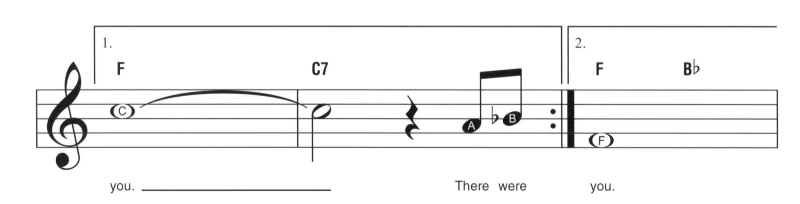

you. _____ There were you.

95

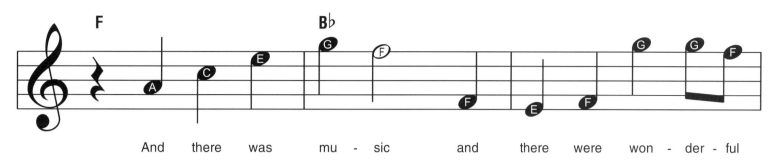

And there was mu - sic and there were won - der - ful

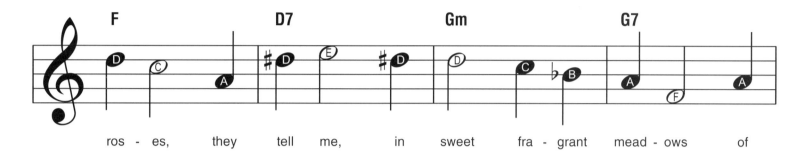

ros - es, they tell me, in sweet fra - grant mead - ows of

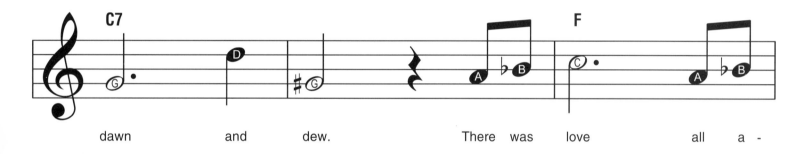

dawn and dew. There was love all a -

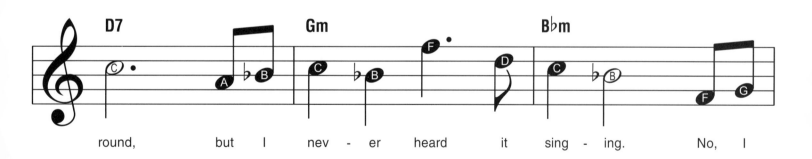

round, but I nev - er heard it sing - ing. No, I

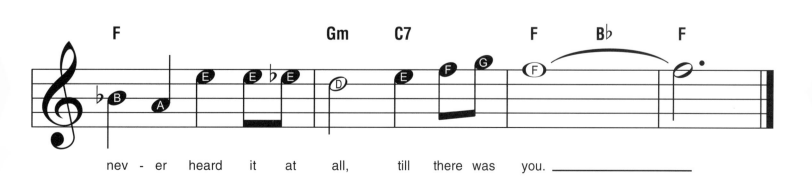

nev - er heard it at all, till there was you. _____

To a Wild Rose
from WOODLAND SKETCHES, OP. 51, NO. 1

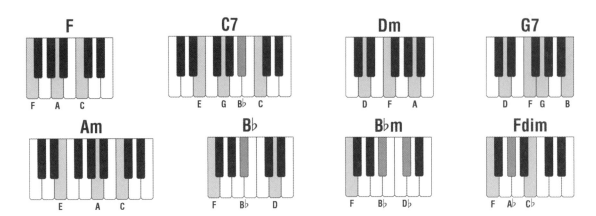

By Edward MacDowell

Slowly, gently

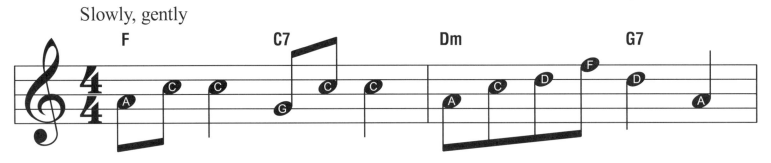

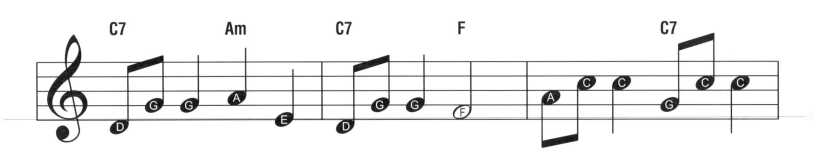

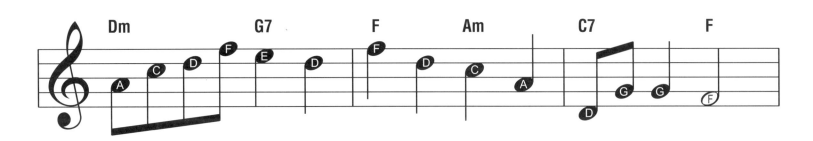

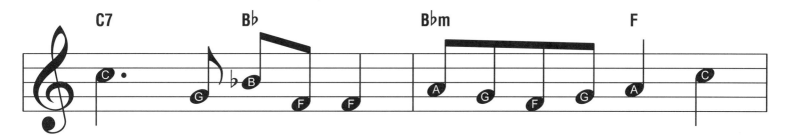

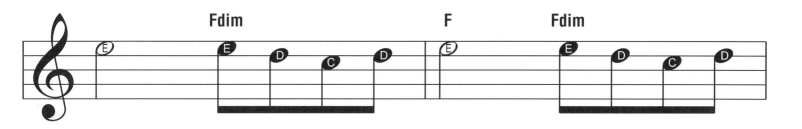

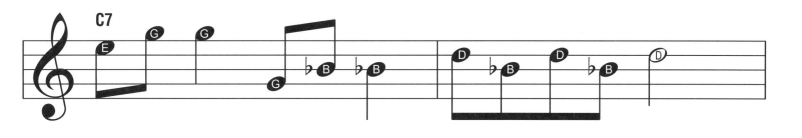

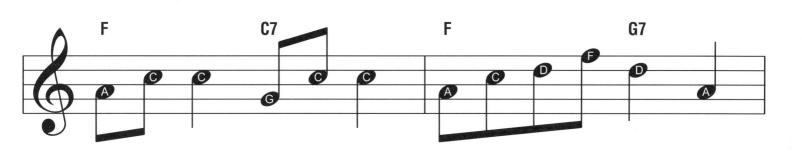

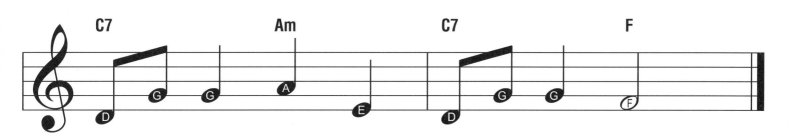

Watermark

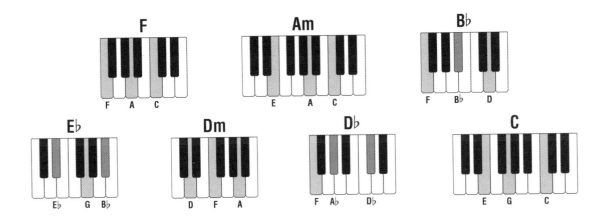

Music by Enya
Words by Roma Ryan

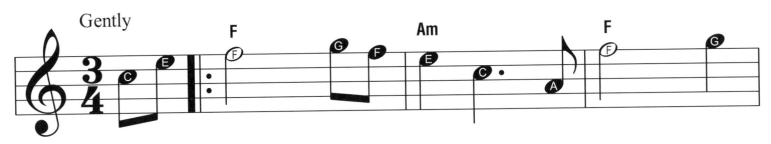

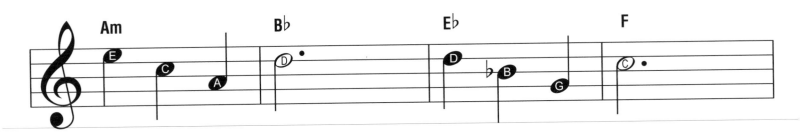

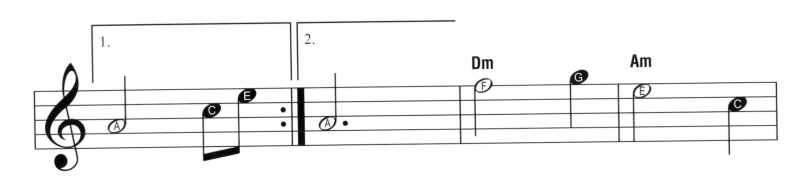

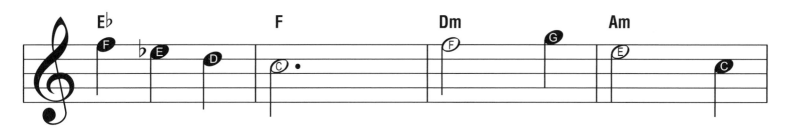

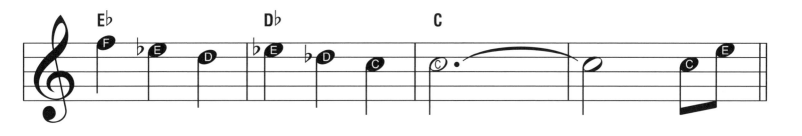

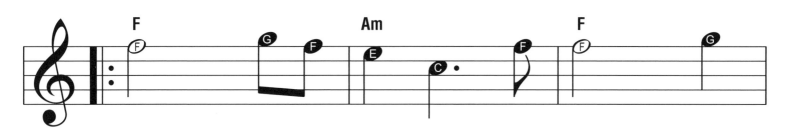

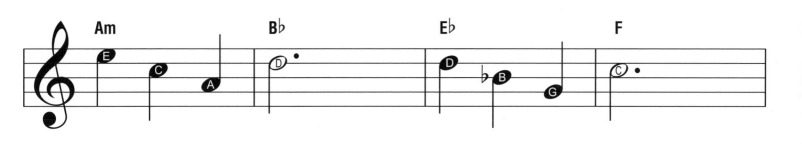

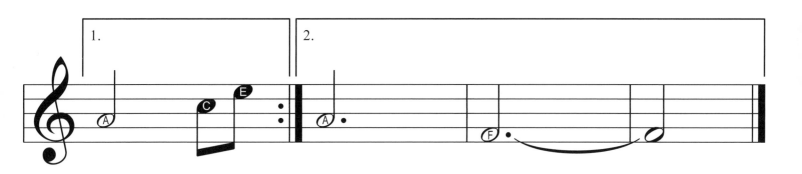

The Way You Look Tonight
from SWING TIME

Words by Dorothy Fields
Music by Jerome Kern

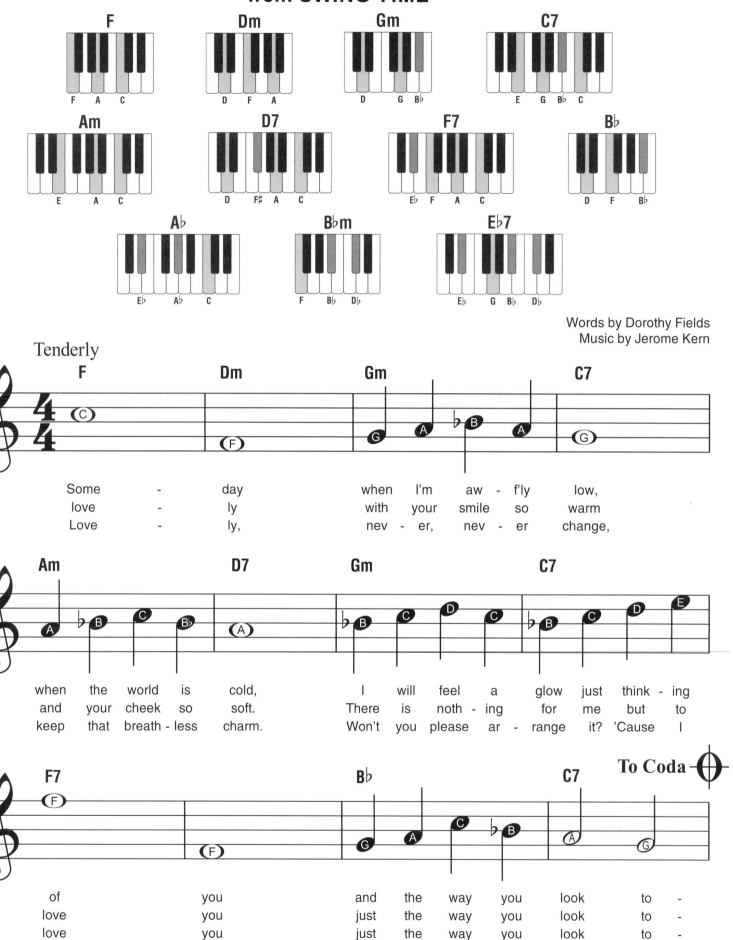

What a Wonderful World

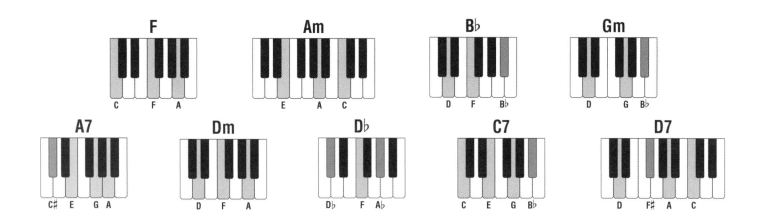

Words and Music by George David Weiss
and Bob Thiele

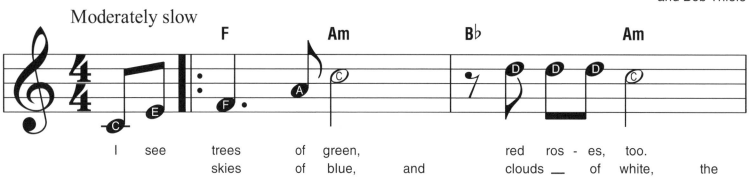

I see trees of green, red ros - es, too.
skies of blue, and clouds __ of white, the

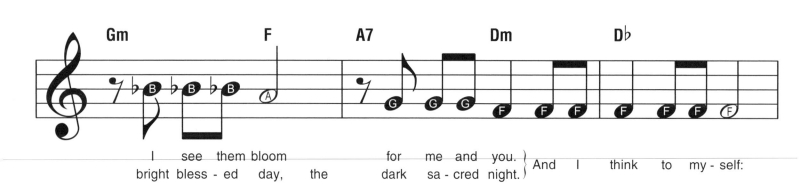

I see them bloom for me and you.
bright bless - ed day, the dark sa - cred night. } And I think to my - self:

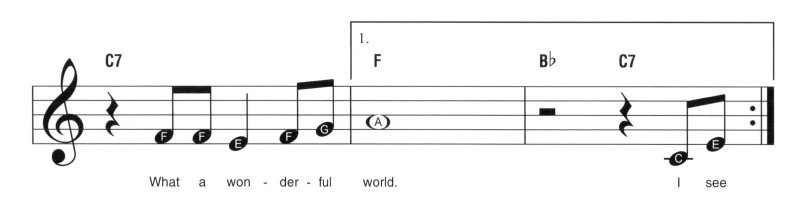

What a won - der - ful world. I see

When She Loved Me

from TOY STORY 2

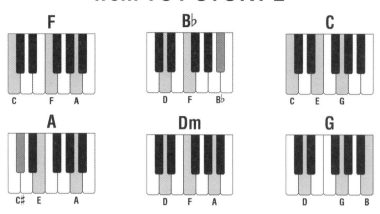

Music and Lyrics by
Randy Newman

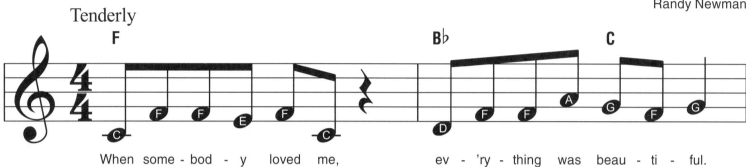

When some - bod - y loved me, ev - 'ry - thing was beau - ti - ful.

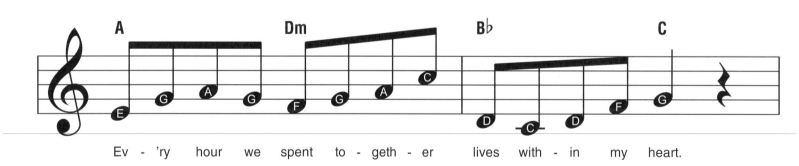

Ev - 'ry hour we spent to - geth - er lives with - in my heart.

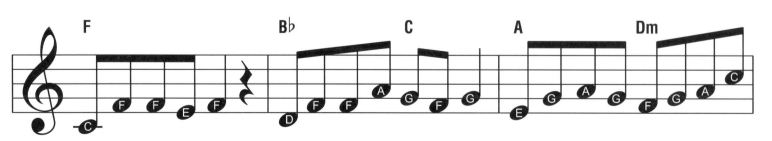

And when she was sad, I was there to dry her tears. And when she was hap - py, so was

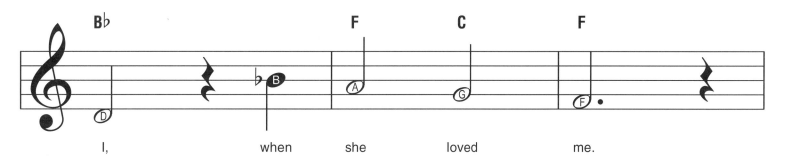

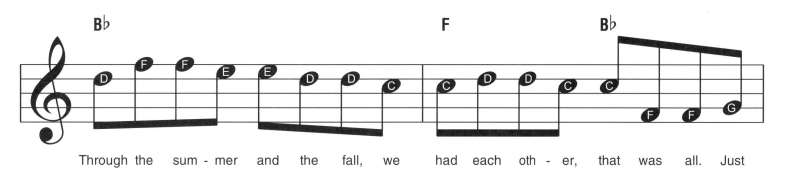

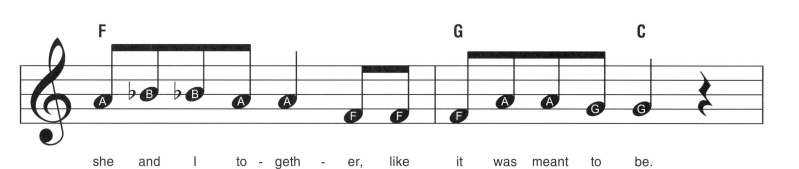

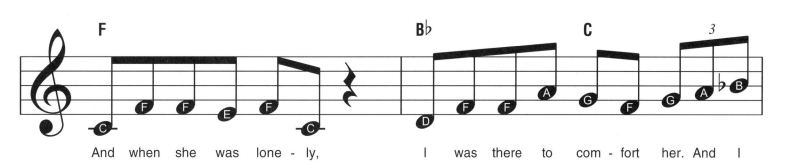

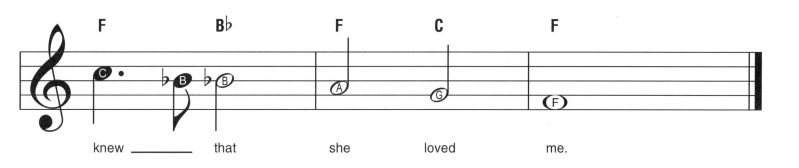

The Wind Beneath My Wings

from the Original Motion Picture BEACHES

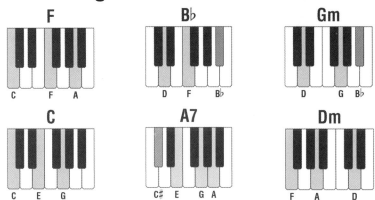

Words and Music by Larry Henley
and Jeff Silbar

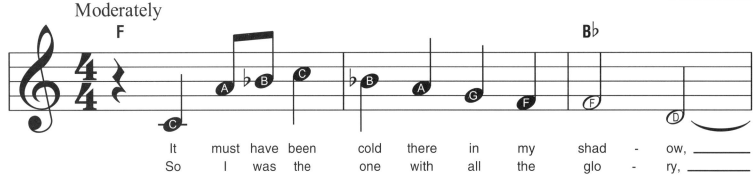

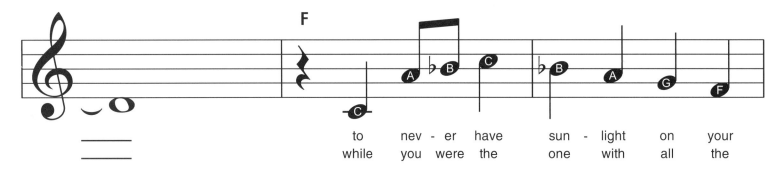

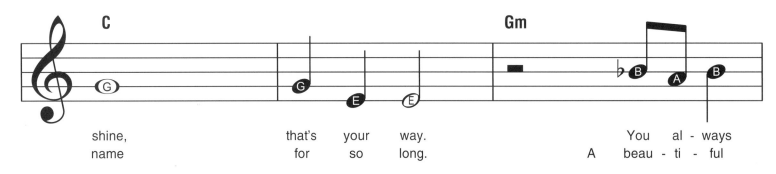

Wonderful Tonight

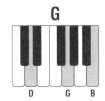
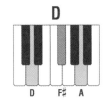
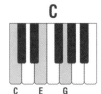

Words and Music by
Eric Clapton

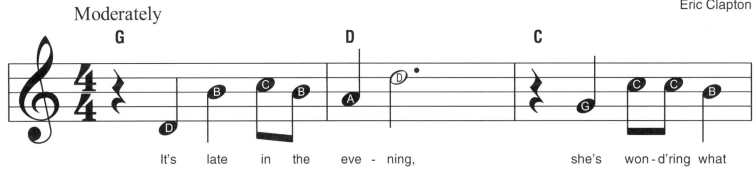

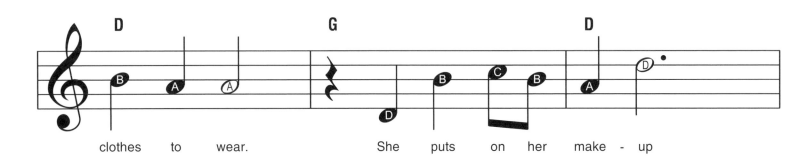

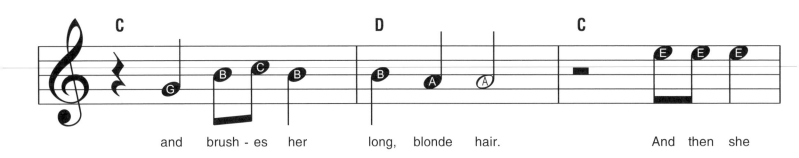

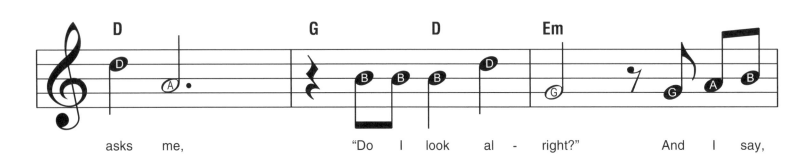

Yesterday

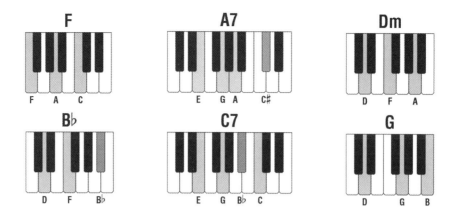

Words and Music by John Lennon
and Paul McCartney

Moderately slow

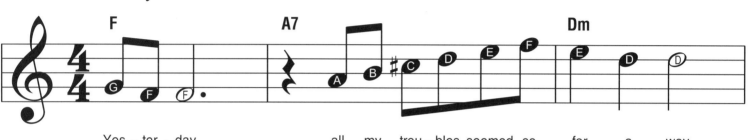

Yes - ter - day, all my trou - bles seemed so far a - way.
Sud - den - ly, I'm not half the man I used to be.

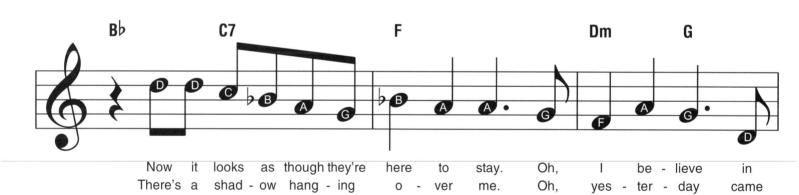

Now it looks as though they're here to stay. Oh, I be - lieve in
There's a shad - ow hang - ing o - ver me. Oh, yes - ter - day came

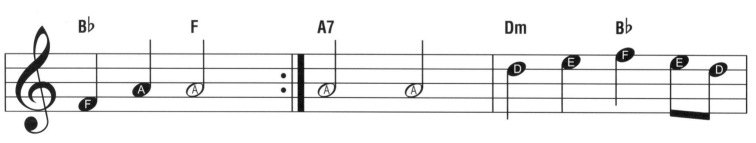

yes - ter - day.
sud - den - ly. Why she had to go, I don't

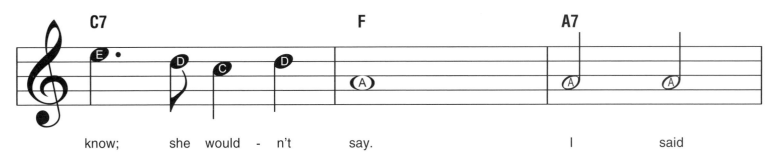

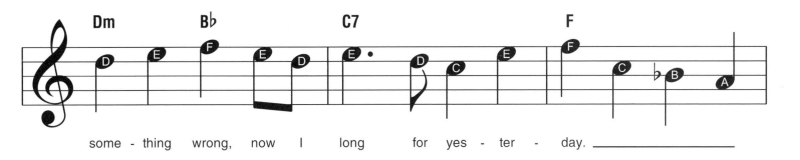

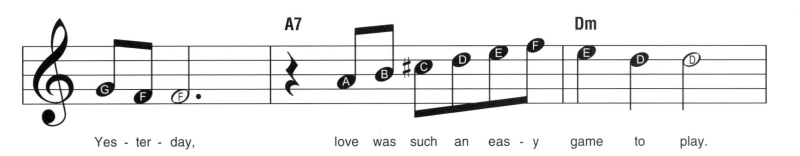

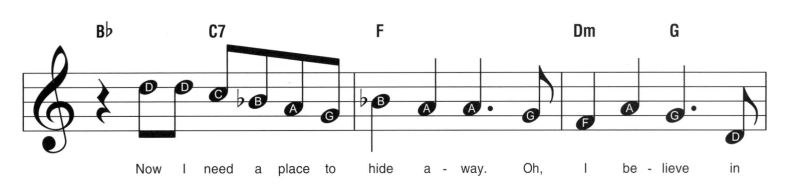

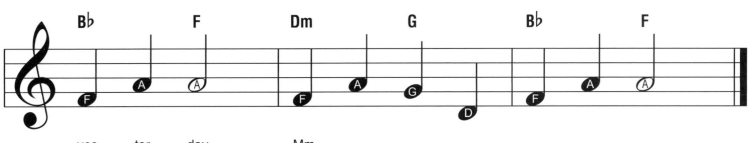

You Are the Reason

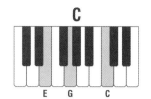
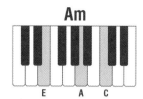
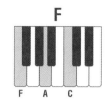
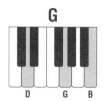
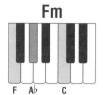

Words and Music by Calum Scott,
Corey Sanders and Jonathan Maguire

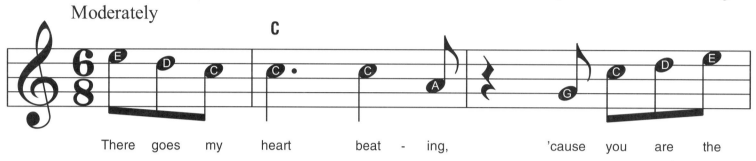

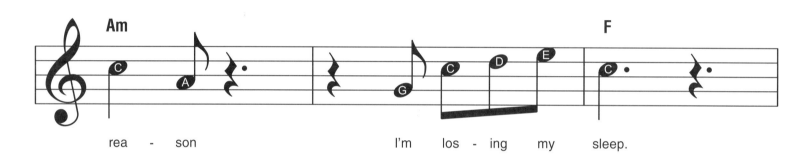

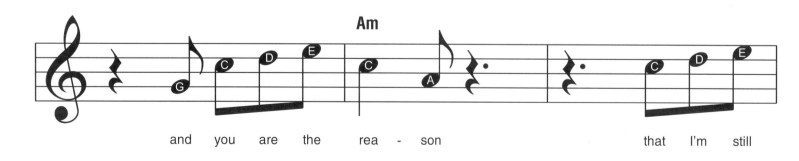

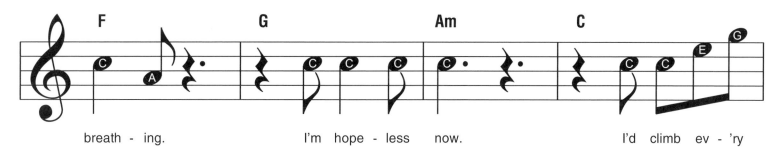

breath - ing.   I'm hope - less now.   I'd climb ev - 'ry

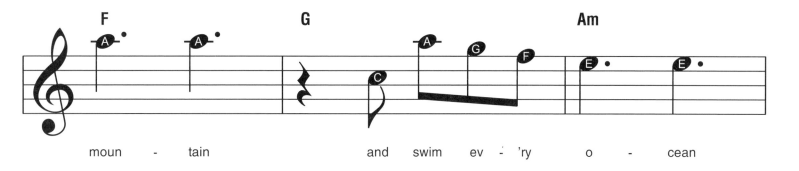

moun - tain   and swim ev - 'ry o - cean

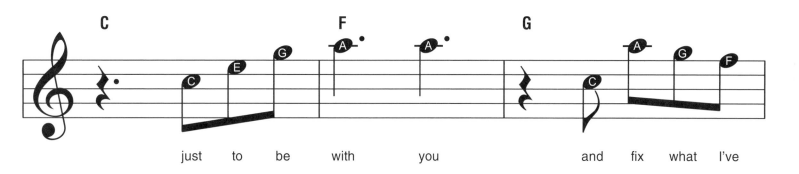

just to be with you   and fix what I've

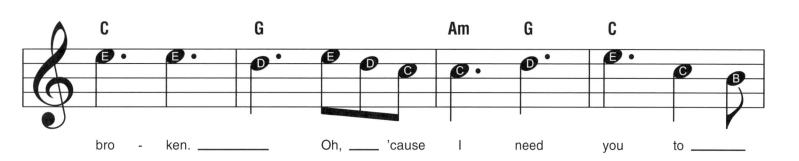

bro - ken. _____ Oh, ___ 'cause I need you to _____

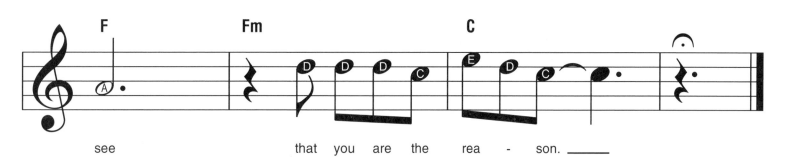

see   that you are the rea - son. _____

You'll Never Walk Alone

from CAROUSEL

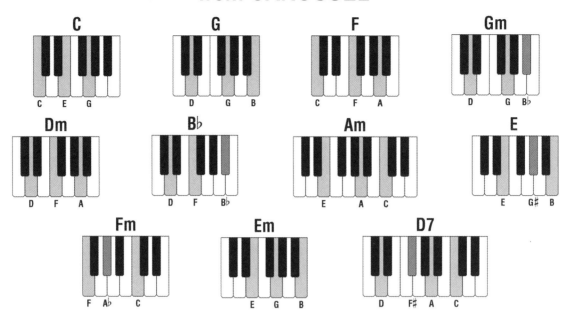

Lyrics by Oscar Hammerstein II
Music by Richard Rodgers

Moderately

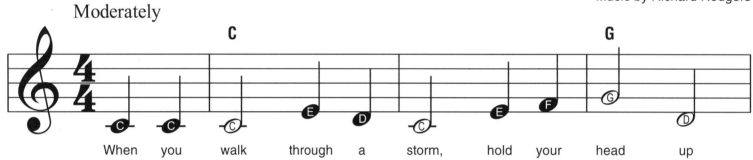

When you walk through a storm, hold your head up

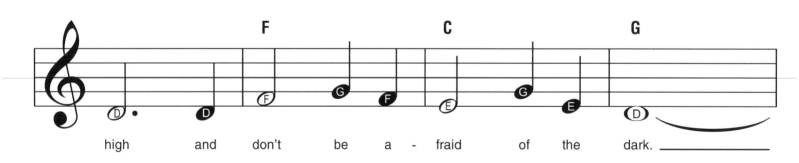

high and don't be a - fraid of the dark. _____

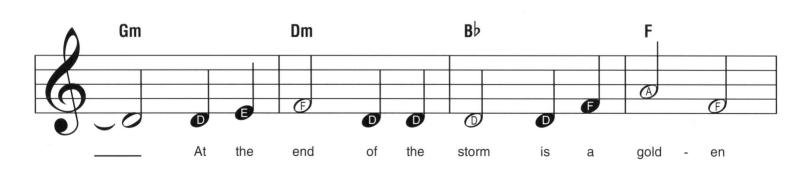

_____ At the end of the storm is a gold - en

You've Got a Friend

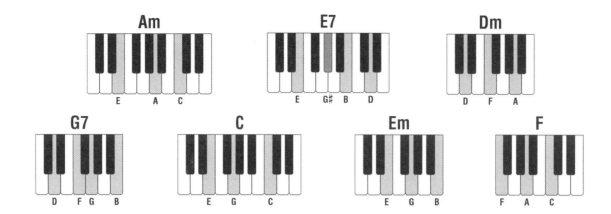

Words and Music by
Carole King

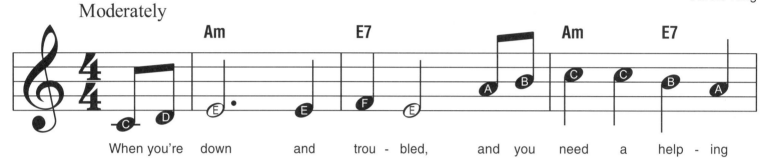

When you're down and trou - bled, and you need a help - ing

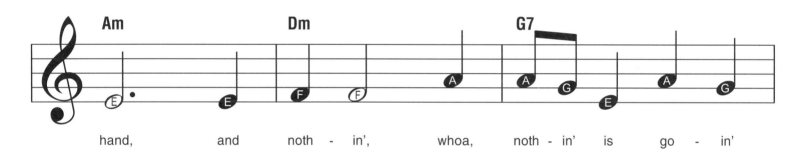

hand, and noth - in', whoa, noth - in' is go - in'

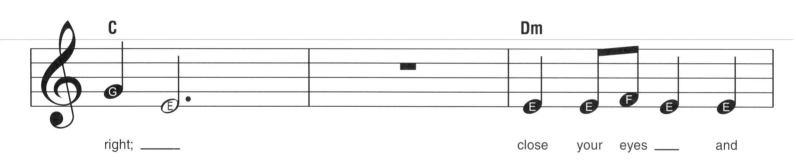

right; _____ close your eyes _____ and

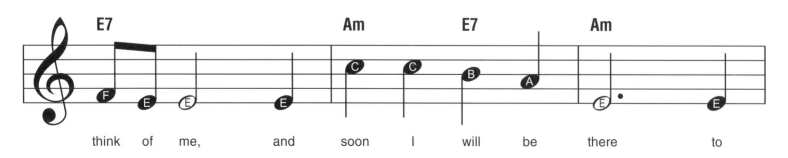

think of me, and soon I will be there to

SUPER EASY SONGBOOK

It's super easy! This series features accessible arrangements for piano, with simple right-hand melody, letter names inside each note, and basic left-hand chord diagrams. Perfect for players of all ages!

THE BEATLES
00198161 60 songs......................$15.99

BEETHOVEN
00345533 21 selections...............$9.99

BEST SONGS EVER
00329877 60 songs......................$15.99

BROADWAY
00193871 60 songs......................$15.99

JOHNNY CASH
00287524 20 songs......................$9.99

CHRISTMAS CAROLS
00277955 60 songs......................$15.99

CHRISTMAS SONGS
00236850 60 songs......................$15.99

CHRISTMAS SONGS WITH 3 CHORDS
00367423 30 songs......................$10.99

CLASSIC ROCK
00287526 60 songs......................$15.99

CLASSICAL
00194693 60 selections...............$15.99

COUNTRY
00285257 60 songs......................$14.99

DISNEY
00199558 60 songs......................$15.99

BOB DYLAN
00364487 22 songs......................$12.99

BILLIE EILISH
00346515 22 songs......................$10.99

FOUR CHORD SONGS
00249533 60 songs......................$15.99

FROZEN COLLECTION
00334069 14 songs......................$10.99

GEORGE GERSHWIN
00345536 22 songs......................$9.99

GOSPEL
00285256 60 songs......................$15.99

HIT SONGS
00194367 60 songs......................$15.99

HYMNS
00194659 60 songs......................$15.99

JAZZ STANDARDS
00233687 60 songs......................$14.99

BILLY JOEL
00329996 22 songs......................$10.99

ELTON JOHN
00298762 22 songs......................$10.99

KIDS' SONGS
00198009 60 songs......................$14.99

LEAN ON ME
00350593 22 songs......................$9.99

THE LION KING
00303511 9 songs......................$9.99

ANDREW LLOYD WEBBER
00249580 48 songs......................$19.99

MOVIE SONGS
00233670 60 songs......................$15.99

PEACEFUL MELODIES
00367880 60 songs......................$16.99

POP SONGS FOR KIDS
00346809 60 songs......................$16.99

POP STANDARDS
00233770 60 songs......................$15.99

QUEEN
00294889 20 songs......................$10.99

ED SHEERAN
00287525 20 songs......................$9.99

SIMPLE SONGS
00329906 60 songs......................$15.99

STAR WARS (EPISODES I-IX)
00345560 17 songs......................$10.99

TAYLOR SWIFT
00323195 22 songs......................$10.99

THREE CHORD SONGS
00249664 60 songs......................$15.99

TOP HITS
00300405 22 songs......................$10.99

WORSHIP
00294871 60 songs......................$15.99

INSTANT Piano Songs

Audio Access Included

The ***Instant Piano Songs*** series will help you play your favorite songs quickly and easily — whether you use one hand or two! Start with the melody in your right hand, adding basic left-hand chords when you're ready. Letter names inside each note speed up the learning process, and optional rhythm patterns take your playing to the next level. Online backing tracks are also included. Stream or download the tracks using the unique code inside each book, then play along to build confidence and sound great!

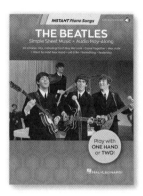

THE BEATLES

All My Loving · Blackbird · Can't Buy Me Love · Eleanor Rigby · Get Back · Here, There and Everywhere · Hey Jude · I Will · Let It Be · Michelle · Nowhere Man · Ob-La-Di, Ob-La-Da · Penny Lane · When I'm Sixty-Four · With a Little Help from My Friends · Yesterday · and more.
00295926 Book/Online Audio.................................$14.99

BROADWAY'S BEST

All I Ask of You · Bring Him Home · Defying Gravity · Don't Cry for Me Argentina · Edelweiss · Memory · The Music of the Night · On My Own · People · Seasons of Love · Send in the Clowns · She Used to Be Mine · Sunrise, Sunset · Tonight · Waving Through a Window · and more.
00323342 Book/Online Audio.................................$14.99

CHRISTMAS CLASSICS

Angels We Have Heard on High · Away in a Manger · Deck the Hall · The First Noel · Good King Wenceslas · Hark! the Herald Angels Sing · Jingle Bells · Jolly Old St. Nicholas · Joy to the World · O Christmas Tree · Up on the Housetop · We Three Kings of Orient Are · We Wish You a Merry Christmas · What Child Is This? · and more.
00348326 Book/Online Audio.................................$14.99

CHRISTMAS STANDARDS

All I Want for Christmas Is You · Christmas Time Is Here · Frosty the Snow Man · Grown-Up Christmas List · A Holly Jolly Christmas · I'll Be Home for Christmas · Jingle Bell Rock · The Little Drummer Boy · Mary, Did You Know? · Merry Christmas, Darling · Rudolph the Red-Nosed Reindeer · White Christmas · and more.
00294854 Book/Online Audio $14.99

CLASSICAL THEMES

Canon (Pachelbel) · Für Elise (Beethoven) · Jesu, Joy of Man's Desiring (Bach) · Jupiter (Holst) · Lullaby (Brahms) · Pomp and Circumstance (Elgar) · Spring (Vivaldi) · Symphony No. 9, Fourth Movement ("Ode to Joy") (Beethoven) · and more.
00283826 Book/Online Audio.................................$14.99

DISNEY FAVORITES

Beauty and the Beast · Can You Feel the Love Tonight · Chim Chim Cher-ee · Colors of the Wind · A Dream Is a Wish Your Heart Makes · Friend Like Me · How Far I'll Go · It's a Small World · Kiss the Girl · Lava · Let It Go · Mickey Mouse March · Part of Your World · Reflection · Remember Me (Ernesto de la Cruz) · A Whole New World · You'll Be in My Heart (Pop Version) · and more.
00283720 Book/Online Audio.................................$14.99

HITS OF 2010-2019

All About That Bass (Meghan Trainor) · All of Me (John Legend) · Can't Stop the Feeling (Justin Timberlake) · Happy (Pharrell Williams) · Hey, Soul Sister (Train) · Just the Way You Are (Bruno Mars) · Rolling in the Deep (Adele) · Shallow (Lady Gaga & Bradley Cooper) · Shake It Off (Taylor Swift) · Shape of You (Ed Sheeran) · and more.
00345364 Book/Online Audio.................................$14.99

KIDS' POP SONGS

Adore You (Harry Styles) · Cool Kids (AJR) · Drivers License (Olivia Rodrigo) · How Far I'll Go (from Moana) · A Million Dreams (from The Greatest Showman) · Ocean Eyes (Billie Eilish) · Shake It Off (Taylor Swift) · What Makes You Beautiful (One Direction) · and more.
00371694 Book/Online Audio.................................$14.99

MOVIE SONGS

As Time Goes By · City of Stars · Endless Love · Hallelujah · I Will Always Love You · Laura · Moon River · My Heart Will Go on (Love Theme from 'Titanic') · Over the Rainbow · Singin' in the Rain · Skyfall · Somewhere Out There · Stayin' Alive · Tears in Heaven · Unchained Melody · Up Where We Belong · The Way We Were · What a Wonderful World · and more.
00283718 Book/Online Audio.................................$14.99

POP HITS

All of Me · Chasing Cars · Despacito · Feel It Still · Havana · Hey, Soul Sister · Ho Hey · I'm Yours · Just Give Me a Reason · Love Yourself · Million Reasons · Perfect · Riptide · Shake It Off · Stay with Me · Thinking Out Loud · Viva La Vida · What Makes You Beautiful · and more.
00283825 Book/Online Audio.................................$15.99

SONGS FOR KIDS

Do-Re-Mi · Hakuna Matata · It's a Small World · On Top of Spaghetti · Puff the Magic Dragon · The Rainbow Connection · SpongeBob SquarePants Theme Song · Take Me Out to the Ball Game · Tomorrow · The Wheels on the Bus · Won't You Be My Neighbor? (It's a Beautiful Day in the Neighborhood) · You Are My Sunshine · and more.
00323352 Book/Online Audio.................................$15.99

HAL•LEONARD®
www.halleonard.com

HAL LEONARD PRESENTS

FAKE BOOKS FOR BEGINNERS!

Entry-level fake books! These books feature larger-than-most fake book notation with simplified harmonies and melodies – and all songs are in the key of C. An introduction addresses basic instruction on playing from a fake book.

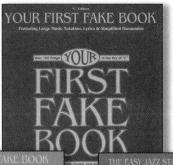 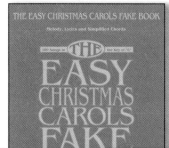 

 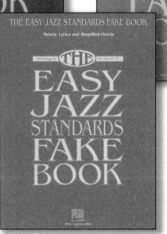 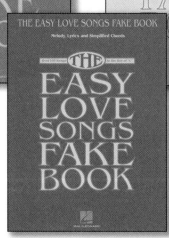 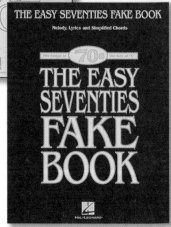

Your First Fake Book
00299529.................................$22.99

The Easy Fake Book
00240144.................................$19.99

The Simplified Fake Book
00299494.................................$22.99

The Beatles Easy Fake Book
00171200.................................$25.00

The Easy Broadway Fake Book
00276670.................................$19.99

The Easy Children's Fake Book
00240428 ....$19.99

The Easy Christian Fake Book
00240328.................................$19.99

The Easy Christmas Carols Fake Book
00238187 ....$19.99

The Easy Christmas Songs Fake Book
00277913.................................$19.99

The Easy Classic Rock Fake Book
00240389 ....$24.99

The Easy Classical Fake Book
00240262.................................$19.99

The Easy Country Fake Book
00240319.................................$22.99

The Easy Disney Fake Book
00275405.................................$24.99

The Easy Folksong Fake Book
00240360.................................$22.99

The Easy 4-Chord Fake Book
00118752 ....$19.99

The Easy G Major Fake Book
00142279 ....$19.99

The Easy Gospel Fake Book
00240169.................................$19.99

The Easy Hymn Fake Book
00240207.................................$19.99

The Easy Jazz Standards Fake Book
00102346.................................$19.99

The Easy Love Songs Fake Book
00159775 ....$24.99

The Easy Pop/Rock Fake Book
00141667 ....$24.99

The Easy 3-Chord Fake Book
00240388 ....$19.99

The Easy Worship Fake Book
00240265.................................$22.99

More of the Easy Worship Fake Book
00240362.................................$22.99

The Easy '20s Fake Book
00240336 ....$19.99

The Easy '30s Fake Book
00240335.................................$19.99

The Easy '40s Fake Book
00240252.................................$19.99

The Easy '50s Fake Book
00240255.................................$22.99

The Easy '60s Fake Book
00240253.................................$22.99

The Easy '70s Fake Book
00240256.................................$22.99

The Easy '80s Fake Book
00240340 ....$24.99

The Easy '90s Fake Book
00240341 ....$19.99

HAL•LEONARD®
halleonard.com

Prices, contents and availability subject to change without notice.